# The End-times Handbook

## Volume 1: Matthew 24 and 25

Buck Hurlbut

All Scriptures are in King James Version unless otherwise noted.
Hurlbut, Buck
    The End-times Handbook: Volume 1: Matthew 24 & 25
ISBN-13: 978-0-9837158-3-2 Softcover
ISBN-13: 978-0-9837158-4-9 Hardcover
ISBN-13: 978-0-9837158-5-6 Kindle
236 Eschatology

Z72022011716447

# Dedication

I want to offer my gratitude to Jesus for His words and for the gift of the indwelling Holy Spirit without Whom I would be abysmally lost in this world. His spiritual gifts, teaching, reminding, convicting, revealing, discerning and peace are lifeblood to me. Thank you for your patience and long-suffering as you interact with my on-going learning.

I want to thank my wife Mary, son Landon and daughter Abby for their support and encouragement. To my wife, thank you for encouraging me to pursue the important and the fulfilling, thank you for bringing joy and gladness these past 28 years; to my daughter, thank you for bringing joy and laughter, thank you for exercising your gift of disarming frustration; and to my son, thank you for the theological dialogs, coffee conversations and for teaching me what you, too, are learning from the Holy Spirit's teaching. I love you all very much.

# Table of Contents

# Acknowledgements

I extend special thanks to Blue Letter Bible for their spectacular app, website and research tools. I cannot fully express my gratitude for the labor you've invested to make God's word and resources so accessible for those of us who love to study. Thank you.

# Introduction

I am a systems analyst who loves to study Scripture. I've been studying systems for 30+ years and Scripture for 40+ years. The conjoining of the two has created some of my most treasured experiences as a follower of Jesus. God has placed an amazing level of intertwining thought in His detailed plan for the salvation of the world. Spanning 7,000 years over multiple people groups, multiple continents, multiple languages, multiple competing enemy factions, multiple world rulers and billions of individual lives, He can keep straight all the moving pieces; He can see how all the entities work together, support each other, define and control each other, contort each other; and ultimately, He can still see the end game. It's truly astounding!

In the following pages, you will find a journey available to the individual who allows Scripture to interpret Scripture, who thinks systemically and who trusts that the Holy Spirit is our teacher. For all that is here, I used only my King James Bible; my Strong's Greek and Hebrew concordance through the treasured Blue Letter Bible app and website; and my own curiosity and intrigue fueled by ongoing revelation at the direction of the Holy Spirit. He really is an amazing adventure guide.

Remember, if God required people to tell us what to believe, that would fully diminish the Holy Spirit's presence and purpose as well as the power of God's word. According to Jesus, the Holy Spirit's mandate is to teach us all things. Remember Jesus' words in John 14:26?

> *26But the Comforter, [which is] the Holy Ghost, whom the Father will send in my name, he shall teach you all things, and bring all things to your remembrance, whatsoever I have said unto you.*

You do *not* need someone to tell you what to believe. A teacher should lead you into discovery so that you can learn on your own. If you are looking to a teacher to know what to believe, and that is stopping you from taking the personal time to learn, you should walk away from your co-dependence and step into a trusting relationship with the Holy Spirit. Your faith and your eternity are too valuable to let an individual or multiple individuals tell you what to believe. A good teacher is going to give you building blocks and compel you in your journey, not lead you to dependence.

If you are listening to end-times teachers so you don't have to study, I hope you'll stop only listening. Get your Bible and use their teaching but compare them to Scripture. Try to disprove them. Don't just accept them. Anyone who tells you that they have the end times figured out and that everyone else is wrong is a teacher from whom to stay away. We never stop learning, and if we are incapable of learning from a 12-year-old child in Sunday school when the Holy Spirit speaks, we need to re-evaluate how we listen. This was the Pharisee's problem when Jesus came to them: they

2

fully missed the Word of God because it was packaged in a 12-year-old boy.

We may individually have much of our understanding correct, but there is always something we can learn from someone else; and just because someone has a PhD in theology may not represent their personal ability to listen to the Holy Spirit. Perhaps the PhD has the mechanics correct, but the degree doesn't mean they have the heart of the Scripture. Degree or no degree, each person is responsible to get the heart of Scripture by engaging it, courting it, and living with it. *You* are the one who needs to find the heart of the Scripture, and you'll do it by reading it on your own, chewing on it, wrestling with it and not giving up until it settles in your heart and spirit. Remember, Jesus told us to ask, seek and knock (Mt 7:7). He wants to be found!

As you enter the following pages, I offer these words from the vantage point of Drew Ray who one day shared with me this refined thought, "If we need a commentary to understand the Scripture, then the Holy Spirit isn't who we've been told. We should be able to drop a copy of the Scripture on an island and with that alone, see the Gospel flourish, or God's word is not what it says it is." I completely agree with Drew. The Holy Spirit is our teacher and He's very good at it. Stop and yield your attention to Him and let Him do his job. Dig in. Don't quit searching. When you feel uneasy or you lack peace in your spirit about something you're reading, question it. Try to disprove everything. After all these, if you have peace and you can't disprove it from Scripture no matter how hard you try, it's likely the truth or close to it. Share what you've gleaned with others. When they disagree, don't just believe them: take their concerns and try to disprove their concerns. If you cannot disprove their concerns, see where you may be wrong. If you can disprove their concerns, hold fast to what you've found and go back and discuss your findings with them. If they get angry, it likely means *they* need to review your concerns because you've pushed against something they can't or don't want to change but are unstable to defend. An anger response is a great way to know we should challenge a belief, study and evaluate it more: when we are angered while trying to defend our core truths, we should ask why, because when we know the truth, it brings peace, rest and stability.

When all is done, remember, you *can* hear the Holy Spirit of God. Ask Him to teach you. Trust that He is teaching you, and don't quit searching.

Enjoy the journey!

Buck Hurlbut

# Start with Jesus

Welcome to one of the most amazing Scripture journeys you may ever encounter. We are venturing together into end-times events. Amazingly, these events appear to be upon us now. Many generations before us have wondered, but I can honestly say that we should not.

We will dive into the Revelation and Daniel quite a lot in the following pages, but we will also follow our intrigue as the study of those books takes us to other places in Scripture. As you read this work and study your copy of the Scripture alongside it, please lay down your preconceived notions of when Jesus may be appearing and the events you believe are beyond dispute. The goal of this work is to let Scripture interpret Scripture. You may have a favorite teacher who says and feels very sincere about their topic; but it doesn't mean they are correct, no matter how much you respect them. I feel very strongly about what is in the pages that follow, but it doesn't mean I'm correct either. All of us who love truth strive for it and can fall short of it. Your job is to discern, to look at the Scripture for yourself and to define your faith according to truth and caution. You *can* understand the Scripture: it's been given to you for that purpose and Jesus' promise to you is that the Holy Spirit will teach you.  In John 14:26, Jesus speaks about the core role of the Holy Spirit in your life, when he says:

> *26But the Comforter, [which is] the Holy Ghost, whom the Father will send in my name, he shall teach you all things, and bring all things to your remembrance, whatsoever I have said unto you.*

The Holy Spirit is here to teach you *all things*, please, give Him room to do so.

The best we can do as teachers is spur you on to search for yourself.  We are past the days when spoon-feeding end-times events is acceptable.  It's time for you to grow into your responsibility if you have not already, to take the time to study these Scriptures for yourself and to see what Scripture represents, because your safety and security, both now and eternally, may very well depend on your dedication to understand the truth on your own. If anyone tells you that you cannot understand what you're reading, if they make a compelling and forceful argument, your job is to assume it's wrong until you can see it in Scripture for yourself and not merely to believe because it's what you want, because you trust the teacher or because it's convenient.

As you embark on the following journey, try to disprove everything. Any of us can "prove" our point in Scripture: we can take a Scripture here and a Scripture there and weave them together to say nearly anything, but when we look at Scripture as a whole and allow it to defend itself and define itself, it can present a different picture.  When we try our best to disprove what we believe, if we cannot, we have even more reason to believe we are correct.  So, if you believe something to be true, try to disprove it from the Scripture. If you can find reason to doubt what you believe to be true, it is likely not solid a solid doctrine and you may need to admit, "I just don't know right now." In those cases, we must find the direction Scripture points, even if it's not to an end we can currently see, and then begin walking that direction, searching for more clarity. And for the record, the word *doctrine* is not a bad word. Sound doctrine, truth that cannot be shaken, is the foundational understanding of our salvation. Paul wrote to Timothy in 1Tim 4:16:

> *16Take heed unto thyself, and unto the doctrine; continue in them: for in doing this thou shalt both save thyself, and them that hear thee.*

Our doctrine is what we believe about anything and how defensible those beliefs are, based on the Scripture. One such item of this type may be your perception of when Jesus will remove the elect out of the earth—the "rapture." You may currently believe Jesus performs this before the tribulation begins, in the middle of the tribulation period, at the end of the tribulation or perhaps at the seventh trumpet of the Revelation. Whatever you may currently believe, if anything, let Scripture try to disprove and define it. Be willing to change if Scripture presents a compelling argument.

The timing of the gathering of the elect to Jesus is just one topic. Others like it are:

- How much of the setup for the end times will the elect experience?
- Will there be a great end-times revival?
- How will we really identify the mark of the beast?

There are lots of questions and would you believe me if I said many of these appear to be plainly answered in the Scripture? You must only be willing to accept what the Scripture says. So, here we go. Are you ready? It seems the best place to begin our journey into the end times is with the person through whom the universe was created. It seems He would have a good view of what lies ahead, and so with that in mind, let's start with Jesus.

## Beginning of the End (Mt 24:1-9)

We begin our journey in Matthew 24:1-2 where Scripture records:

> *¹And Jesus went out, and departed from the temple: and his disciples came to him for to show him the buildings of the temple. ²And Jesus said unto them, See ye not all these things? Verily I say unto you, There shall not be left here one stone upon another that shall not be thrown down.¹*

Jesus begins by telling the disciples a future event: the temple they love so much, where they come regularly to fulfill their sacrificial duties to God and without which they cannot imagine worshiping God, is to be fully destroyed, down to the ground, with no stone left upon another. Interestingly, this topic of temple worship remains key to the timing of all major events of the end times. Could this be why Jesus brings up the topic? The full destruction of the temple is of grave concern to the disciples and, after pondering for a while, they later have a conversation with Jesus that begins in verse three:

> *³And as he [Jesus] sat upon the mount of Olives, the disciples came unto him privately, saying, Tell us,*

---

¹ The Jewish historian Josephus discusses how the Jerusalem temple destruction fully happens at the fall of Jerusalem in the hands of the Roman empire (Josephus, War of the Jews, 7:1:1).

*when shall these things be? And what shall be the*
*sign of thy coming, and of the end of the world?*

From their question, we see there must have been more that was discussed because they identified a level of severity they expected to occur. They ask Jesus: 1) When shall these things [the temple's destruction] be? 2) What shall be the sign of your coming? and 3) [What shall be the sign] of the end of the world? I'm always fascinated by concepts Scripture *doesn't* say but that likely exist behind the words. We should note that the disciples associated a sequence of events: destruction of the temple, Jesus' return then the end of the world. Somehow, the disciples had a sense of timing in their question because they were able to formulate what they thought would happen and the sequence in which it would happen. It's from this vantage point that we enter Jesus' end-times conversation in Matthew chapters 24 and 25.

Before we go any further, let me underscore that it is not my intent to exhaust the study of Scripture on this topic. I am convinced that anyone willing to spend time could invest the entirety of their life pursuing the detailed, end-times plan of God for mankind. Here however, our goal is to understand where we are, what lies ahead, how to prepare for things coming on the world, what signs to watch for that tell us where we are and how to live properly to face Jesus at our coming to Him or His return to us. Whether every end-times event happens in our lifetime or not, our response is the same: live a life prepared to meet God and Jesus face to face so we are not ashamed when we look into Their eyes. We need to allow Scripture to guide our journey and preparation; with these understandings at the forefront, let's see what Jesus explains.

*Deception Begins*

Interestingly, the very first thing Jesus says to the disciples is "Take heed that no man deceive you" (Mt 24:4). Of all things that Jesus could say to the disciples in response to their questions of: When will the temple be destroyed? When will you return? When will the world end? Jesus, the Word of God Himself, responds with, "Take heed that no man deceive you." The words "take heed" mean *to consider and weigh carefully*[2] and I would say *get your perception right*. I think this underscores the value of Jesus' response! It wasn't that the destruction of the temple was inconsequential, or that His return wasn't valuable or that the end of the world wasn't worth discussing; it was that the coming deception was a threat that could distort the listener's ability to rightly judge everything else Jesus would discuss.

Jesus tells us to start with the basics, to get our perception right, to find what reality is; and we must understand that in absence of a love and pursuit of the truth, the rest of the end-times events won't matter because we will miss them or become victim to them. **We will love truth, or we will believe a lie**. This understanding is preeminent in Jesus' answer to the disciples: without this basis, the rest of His conversation will not have a proper foundation because deception will abound in the end times. Let's see how the apostle Paul discusses this same topic: he seemingly understood Jesus' words.

Journey over to 2Thes 2 and start with the beginning of the chapter:

---

[2] βλέπω pronounced blep'-o (Strongs G991)

*[1]Now we beseech you, bretheren, by the coming of our Lord Jesus Christ, and by our gathering together unto him, [2]That ye be not soon shaken in mind, or be troubled, neither by spirit, nor by word, nor by letter as from us, as that the day of Christ is at hand. [3]Let no man deceive you by any means: for that day shall not come, except there come a falling away first, and that man of sin be revealed, the son of perdition[3]; [4]who opposeth and exalteth himself above all that is called God, or that is worshipped; so that he as God sitteth in the temple of God, showing himself that he is God.*

As we look at Paul's words, and for the rest of this writing, I will not use the word "rapture" because, frankly, it is my perception that it has come to represent many different interpretations and arguments, and I want us to let Scripture interpret Scripture. Many people can find Scripture to defend what they believe, even if it means a quick twist here or there. **Our goal must be to try and disprove our beliefs. Only if we cannot disprove our beliefs do we really have a reason to believe they may be true.**

In 2Thes 2, Paul is predicating his conversation about deception on the coming of Jesus and the gathering of the elect of God to Him. In verse three, Paul starts by saying "Let no man deceive you by any means...." Paul understood Jesus' concern: deception will abound in the end days the

---

[3] The phrase "son of perdition" is only used twice in scripture: here and in Jn 17:12. This is very important as we will experience later.

closer we get to those events. How is it that Paul begins in 2Thes 2:1?

> *¹Now we beseech you, brethren, by the coming of our Lord Jesus Christ, and by our gathering together unto him….*

Paul tells us that what he is about to discuss has everything to do with two points: 1) the coming of our Lord Jesus Christ and 2) our being gathered together to Him. It's interesting that Paul puts our gathering to Jesus after His coming, isn't it? It is also interesting that Paul includes himself and the entire church as the objects being gathered to Jesus: there is no subset of believers or category of Jesus followers being discussed – it is all believers. We must ask why?

Perhaps you believe that the elect of God being gathered together to meet Jesus happens very early in the end-times sequence, but what else does Paul say must happen?

> *³Let no man deceive you by any means: for that day shall not come, except there come a falling away first, and that man of sin be revealed, the son of perdition….*

There must be a great falling away and the man of sin must be revealed. According to Scripture, these too must happen before the coming of Jesus.

Our goal is to let Scripture interpret Scripture, so we need to file this away. Write it on a card, write it in a notebook, but put it somewhere so we don't lose any connecting information moving forward. When we have notable points, I will mark them like this:

**The Day of Jesus' Return** – In 2Thes 2:1-4, the apostle Paul identifies this sequence about the coming of Jesus and our gathering to Him: "that day" will not happen until 1) there is a great falling away and 2) the man of sin be revealed.

Now remember what brought us here: Jesus answered the disciples' questions about the end of the temple, His return and the end of the world by saying, "Take heed that no man deceive you." Here in 2Thes 2, also speaking about Jesus coming and the end of the world, Paul writes "Let no man deceive you." Do you see a theme? There is much in 2Thes 2 we could discuss, but let's fast forward to verses 8-12:

> *8And then shall that Wicked [man] be revealed, whom the Lord shall consume with the spirit of his mouth, and shall destroy with the brightness of his coming: 9Even him, whose coming is after the working of Satan with all power and signs and lying wonders. 10And with all deceivableness of unrighteousness in them that perish: because they received not the love of the truth that they might be saved. 11And for this cause God shall send them strong delusion, that they should believe a lie: 12That they all might be damned who believed not the truth, but had pleasure in unrighteousness.*

Paul helps us understand: the wicked one who will come (a description of the beast-man of the Revelation, the end-days king of prophecy known for *the mark of the beast*) will be first revealed (v. 8) and then that wicked man will be destroyed by Jesus (v. 8). This man of wickedness comes

13

bringing with him the works resembling satan [sic.][4] showing power with signs and lying wonders. This person will be extremely skilled at deception; he will make deception look like the truth so that it's very difficult to see the difference. Here, though, is the catch: this deception will happen in people "because they received not the love of the truth that they might be saved" (v. 10).

Paul is pointing out the individual responsibility of every member of humankind: a love for the truth. If we do not have a love for the truth, we will not be saved: we will be deceived. **We must love the truth to see the lie.** How do we know if we love the truth? Any of us can say, "Sure I love the truth!" but how do we know? Our deeds show our heart, so the question we must answer is: **What am I doing that proves I love the truth? How am I gaining the truth so that I can see the lie?** Take a moment to respond: Will you?

### Loving the Truth

I'm reminded of an example in my life where loving the truth exposed the lie. When I was younger, I worked as a cashier at a Food Barn grocery store in Kansas. I handled money all day long, both taking it from customers and returning it to them. Every day, I would touch $1s, $5s, $10s, $20s and some $100s. Now, with certainty, I touched more $1s and $5s than any other denomination of bills, but all money has one source of truth: they are all made the same way from the same materials and by the same organization: they are consistent. One day, I was pulling money from my

---

[4] Through the entirety of this work, I have purposefully chosen to use the lower-case spelling, proper name notwithstanding, for satan and any demon names. There is no recognition due any of these names. However, I do not adjust the biblical text.

till to return change. I pulled out a stack of $5s because it seems I was out of $10s and $20s at that moment; and as I was counting them mindlessly, I hit a bill that felt strangely unfamiliar: something was wrong because it didn't feel like the ones before it. Instantaneously, I set the $5 aside and kept counting. When the checkout line had died down, I looked at the "$5" and realized it was not a familiar $5: it was a silver certificate from the early 1900's. I knew instantly that the bill was not normal; I could feel it; something was wrong, and I knew something was wrong because I had touched thousands of consistent $5 bills before that. I didn't have to overthink it; it was instinctive and natural: even though that $5 silver certificate was the same size, basic color palate and had "5" in the corners, without looking at the bill, I knew it wasn't a true $5 bill.

How are we loving the truth? Are we touching it every day? Are we training ourselves how it feels? Are we using it in our daily lives? Are we reading it daily in the Scriptures? Are we hearing it from God directly as we spend time with Him? **What are we doing daily, that we can observe in our own lives, that proves to us we have a love for the truth that is more than just our own self-confirming belief?** Stop and write a list for yourself. If you observe yourself from the outside, what can you say you are doing to touch the truth and to become very familiar with it so that you can spot deception? We need to take a strong account here because our eternity rests on this, so we must be certain! No one can take us out of the hands of God if we have stepped in, but we are fully able to step out of our own free will. Judas Iscariot, the once disciple of Jesus who later betrayed him to death, is proof of this as we observe in John 13 and John 17; we see this covered in other Scriptures as well (2Thes 2, 2Tim 2 among a few). We must love the truth and dedicate ourselves to the death to pursue it and never let go of it.[5]

*Normal is Not Necessarily Truth*

We need to understand that truth is often defined, understood and believed by perception. In other words, something can seem to be the truth but not be the truth. Every day, we allow our definition of truth to be affected by our culture, by our own experiences and by myriad other influences. If you are a fan of pornography, R-rated thrillers, soaps, romance novels, hall and mark movies or adult cartoons, you likely believe that sex and relationships are something they are not, because you've allowed a fictional representation to affect your perception of reality; you've allowed what is not truth to shape truth for you. You may think you've somehow protected yourself from their effects, but do any of these media stir up a desire inside you? Do you smile or watch intently when watching them? Do they conjure up emotional or physical response? You wouldn't watch or read these items if they didn't do something for you: you get something out of them that meets some personal pleasure or desire. Maybe you watch a weekly sitcom, binge watch seasons of a show or read certain books with witchcraft. Any time we allow something to meet a desire inside us, we invite an adjustment to our perception of truth.

The same observations can be made about money: you likely believe money can be spent according to rules of poverty. For you, poverty may be the mindset that you must

---

[5] We will discuss laying down our salvation elsewhere. We cannot be plucked out of Jesus' hand, but we can step out of it willingly if we choose.

not spend, irrespective of how much you earn, because you never know if it will be available later. Your rule of poverty may be that you have no poverty, and you can spend what you want when you want because you have so much. Your rule of poverty may be that you allow yourself 10% for personal spending and after that, the rest is untouchable. Where did you derive that "truth"? What about use of social drugs like alcohol, cigarettes and marijuana or your perception of politics? Every one of these depends on you relying on some kind of "truth"; something that drives meaning; something that should be immobile and something upon which you're staking your life.

Even good entertainment can lead us away from the truth. How do you form your understanding of the Old Testament accounts? If I asked you to tell me the account of Joseph or Moses, would you immediately resort to your memory of Scripture? Or would you immediately begin with a movie you saw and start from there? How do you separate the two? I'm amazed at the number of people who allow the movie industry to define their definition of truth, and by the way, I'm even more amazed at how I have allowed it in my own life and I'm very vigilant against gaining truth from movies. I *really* watch that I don't allow it, to the point that I often have my Bible open while watching a movie to keep myself in check and yet just the other day, I caught a "fact" that I believed was truth but that was from a movie and not in Scripture.

We *must* be careful not to allow "normal" to equal "truth." Normal is only normal to you and to those who agree with you. You typically group yourself with others who feel generally the same as you and who see life the way you do because being too far from *normal* is uncomfortable and hard to maintain. When we find ourselves in the abnormal, we struggle to know what to do, how to interact, what to say or not say, and we become very self-conscious. Living that way takes too much thought and time. We rely on *normal* to give us a sense of safety and stability, a sense of belonging. We will seek normal at all costs. What is abnormal is what we disagree with and how far that disagreement veers from our perceptions and convictions. If we allow "normal" to be the truth, we may allow ourselves to slip more and more away from truth because normal changes as culture changes and can be defined by our surroundings and relationships.

Let me offer one last illustration to drive home the observation that normal changes and how we change with it. In the 1940s, TV would *never* show a husband and wife in the same bed: it was socially unacceptable. Now, we see not only husbands and wives in bed together, but we also see men with men and women with women, acting out sexual acts in front of us—even if no skin is showing. In the 1950s it was not acceptable to see a navel on TV. Old sitcoms like Gilligan's Island and I Dream of Jeannie were rated down severely by the public if the actresses exposed her navel. Until 1973, same-sex attraction was considered a type of mental disorder and now it is encouraged professionally, medically, socially and in the entertainment industry. If we allow normal to define truth, we will move toward destruction.

The Greek language defines truth as "the highest form of reality that exists.[6]" John the apostle records Jesus' words in John 14:6:

---

[6] ἀλήθεια pronounced as al-ay'-thi-a (Strongs G225)

*⁶I am the way, the truth and the life. No one comes
to the Father but by me.*

Jesus is "the truth" and anything we accept that is not
according to His character, His words and His life is false—
non-truth. Porn is non-truth and yet it will define the
mindset of many reading these words. Entertainment is
typically non-truth, and a constant diet of immoral social
unions may lead us to believe that marriage is something it's
not or that sex, relationships and love are something they are
not. An abundance of money without an understanding of
truth will open the door to buy boats, trucks, and larger than
necessary houses because we want them; and yet, if we look
at all these from the lens of truth, we may feel differently.
In Luke 18:22 we read:

*²²Now when Jesus heard these things, he said unto
him, Yet lackest thou one thing: sell all that thou
hast, and distribute unto the poor, and thou shalt
have treasure in heaven: and come, follow me.*

If you stop and think about this, would you agree that
having treasure in Heaven that is eternal, where you will see
it for billions of years, is important? Would you agree that
having something precious to give Jesus when you see Him
face to face is important? Would you agree that since Jesus
said these words, they are important? Do you believe Jesus
meant these words when saying them? If Jesus spoke these
words, are they the truth? Does Jesus always tell the truth?
Can we trust these words? Now…Are you doing them? Are
you selling all you have and giving to the poor? You likely
just agreed these words are true, important and eternal, yet
we will likely also agree and say, "I'm not doing this" and
yet, depending on how honest we want to be with ourselves,

we might say our current lifestyles are normal. We trade *normal* for *truth* every day. What are we doing to stop this deception and to correct our lives?

---

**Prophecy Watch**: We cannot allow *normal* to equal *truth*. If we do, we will be swept away in deception. We *must* know God's word, His truth and be willing to judge ourselves and change to live the truth.

---

Why have I focused so much on this topic? Because this is *exactly* what Jesus and Paul are warning us about. "Be not deceived" and "love the truth." These two go hand in hand, and unless we are willing to take an honest look at our lives, we may be allowing our culture, our lust and our greed to define our truth instead of allowing truth to show us our culture, lust and greed.

*The Beginning of Sorrows and Birth Pangs*

There is so much more we could discuss in 2Thes 2, but for now let's go back to what Jesus is saying in Mt 24. Jesus is being asked by His disciples about the destruction of the temple, His coming and the end of the world. Jesus replies with a truth that is foundational to everything else He's about to explain, and I don't believe it's the answer the disciples were expecting. Jesus says, "Take heed that no man deceive you" then he continues in Mt 24:5-8:

> *⁵For many shall come in my name, saying, I am Christ; and shall deceive many. ⁶And ye shall hear of wars and rumors of wars: see that ye be not troubled: for all these things must come to pass, but the end is not yet. ⁷For nation shall rise against nation, and kingdom against kingdom: and there shall be famines, and pestilences, and earthquakes,*

*in diverse places. ⁸All these are the beginning of sorrows.*

Jesus continues by telling the disciples that when deception increases in the end times, there will be several people who are believable Christ-like personalities, and these will deceive many. Jesus says they "will come in my name" which in the Greek is the same as saying: they will come in my authority, deeds, commands, excellence and my apparent character[7]. Whom will these people in Jesus' character come and deceive? Those who do not love the truth, as we just learned.

Jesus then explains that during, and on the heels of, the increased deception, legitimate wars and rumors of wars will arise and that this will be the norm but that the end is not yet. Again, it's very interesting to consider what Scripture says without saying it. Jesus tells us "And ye shall hear of wars and rumors of wars: see that you be not troubled: for…the end is not yet." What didn't Jesus say here but that He's pointing out? These wars and rumors of wars will make us think that the end is here, but it's not. These wars and rumors will be so destructive or believably destructive, that we will naturally think, "This is it! It's over. The world is coming to an end." We will naturally *want* to believe that the end is happening because of the cataclysmic threat of these wars and rumors.

These wars aren't just between countries. The phrase "nation shall rise against nation" does, indeed, mean country against country; but the phrase "kingdom against kingdom" means factions inside countries. We will see wars and civil

---

[7] ὄνομα pronounced on'-om-ah (Strongs G3686)

outbreaks between countries and inside countries. Still, Jesus says, this isn't the end: "All these are the beginning of sorrows" (v. 8). The phrase "the beginning of sorrows" can also be translated, "the beginning of birth pangs.[8]" Interestingly, Jesus uses a word here that can mean the onset of childbirth. Let's look at another place where this Greek word is used.

If we turn to 1 Thes 4:13 and read through 1 Thes 5:3, we see the following well known and loved scripture:

> *1Thes4:13But I would not have you to be ignorant, brethren, concerning them which are asleep, that ye sorrow not, even as others which have no hope. 14For if we believe that Jesus died and rose again, even so them also which sleep in Jesus will God bring with him. 15For this we say unto you by the word of the Lord, that we which are alive and remain unto the coming of the Lord shall not prevent them which are asleep. 16For the Lord himself shall descend from heaven with a shout, with the voice of the archangel, and with the trump of God: and the dead in Christ shall rise first: 17Then we which are alive and remain shall be caught up together with them in the clouds to meet the Lord in the air: and so shall we ever be with the Lord. 18Wherefore comfort one another with these words.*
>
> *5:1But of the times and the seasons, brethren, ye have no need that I write unto you. 2For yourselves know perfectly that the day of the Lord so cometh as a thief*

---

[8] ὠδίν pronounced as o-deen' (Strongs G5604)

*in the night. ³For when they shall say, Peace and safety: then sudden destruction cometh upon them, as travail upon a woman with child; and they shall not escape.*

In context, we are talking about the appearing of Jesus and the elect being gathered to Him in the clouds. Paul states we should comfort each other with the fact it will happen and then Paul immediately begins speaking about the "times and the seasons" for the "day of the Lord." He's explaining in chapter five verse three that when the time comes, it will happen "…as travail upon a woman with child." The word for "travail" here in 1Thes 4 and for "sorrows" in Mt 24 is the identical word (Gk. ὠδὶν[9] – ōdin).

Jesus says that nation will rise against nation, kingdom against kingdom, there will be plagues, pestilences and earthquakes in diverse places and that these are the *beginning* of the time of sorrows. Paul discusses the same time frame and states it will bring destruction as travail upon a woman with child. Paul notes that when it begins, it will continue to escalate with peaks and troughs like childbirth where the birth pangs happen, then rest; then harder pains, then less rest; then harder and longer pains, then some rest but less still until we reach the point of birth where the pains are the most intense and there is nearly no rest between contractions. Both Jesus' account and Paul's account use the same Greek word to explain the end-times events. We will return to spend more time on the scriptures in 1 and 2 Thessalonians, but for now, the takeaway is this:

---

[9] ὠδίν pronounced as o-deen' (Strongs G5604)

**The Time of Sorrows** – the end-times events will be prefaced with times of difficulty and rest that escalates like childbirth, becoming more painful and longer in duration, until it's exhausting and overwhelming and there is no way out but through it (1 Thes 4:13-5:3).

Jesus says, "All these are the beginning of sorrows" (Mt 24:8) as a way of letting us know that we are just entering the start of something big and that this is not the end, but the *beginning*.

The next word Jesus uses is "Then...." Jesus says, "Then shall they deliver you up to be afflicted and shall kill you: and ye shall be hated of all nations for my name's sake" (Mt 24:9). When we see the word "then" have to ask ourselves a minimum of two questions: 1) does *then* mean sequence such as "I'm going to the store then to work" or 2) does "then" mean "at some point or place in time" without reference to position in the current sequence, but as an insert somewhere in the past or future, such as "I am going to drive three hours from Oklahoma City to Dallas; then I will make some calls because the trip is long and I need something to do." In the first example, I offered a sense of sequence. In the second example, I gave the entire storyline (i.e., the drive from Oklahoma City to Dallas) and once you knew the story, I inserted specific details about what I would do sometime during the journey ("then"). When we see the word "then" in these accounts, we must figure out which way the word is being used, because it may change the meaning significantly; and the only way we can tell how it's used is in context. Let's look at the context here in Matthew 24:9.

If we evaluate Jesus words from Mt. 24:4 through Mt 24:8, Jesus gives us the following points in sequence:

1. Take heed that no man deceives you.
2. Many will come in my name saying I am Christ.
3. Many will be deceived.
4. You will hear of wars and rumors of wars.
5. Be not troubled.
6. These things must happen, but the end is not yet.
7. Nations shall fight.
8. Kingdoms shall fight.
9. Famines, pestilences and earthquakes will happen.
10. *ALL* these are the beginning of sorrows.

Jesus tells us that all these events constitute the beginning of sorrows, not just one or two of them, but all of them combined define the "beginning of sorrows." Jesus also tells us that since these are the "beginning," there are more sorrows after these events that Jesus isn't yet telling us (think "beginning" vs. "end"). Unfortunately, this Scripture alone doesn't offer enough context to know if "then" means "in the midst of these" like the trip from Oklahoma City to Dallas or "as a consequence of these" like the example of going to the store and then going to work; so, we will need to look at Mark and Luke to see if they cover this topic and can shed some additional light.

Mark's gospel records this conversation in Mk 13:5-11. Here, Mark records his understanding of the conversation in the following few verses starting in verse eight:

> *[8]For nation shall rise against nation, and kingdom against kingdom: and there shall be earthquakes in diverse places, and there shall be famines and troubles: these are the beginnings of sorrows. [9]But take heed to yourselves: for they shall deliver you up to councils; and in the synagogues ye shall be*

*beaten: and ye shall be brought before rulers and kings for my sake, for a testimony against them.*

In Mark's gospel, he ties the beginning of sorrows directly into the sequence, moving immediately into "but take heed to yourselves." Interestingly, starting the sentence with "but" only means to consider what has just been said and in contrast to the previous understanding, make a decision: i.e., the beginning of sorrows will happen, but take heed. This also only gives us a piece of the puzzle: that somewhere in the beginning of sorrows, we are to take note. So, let's see what Luke has to say. To find Luke's account, we turn to Luke 21:8-12 which reads:

*⁸And he said, Take heed that ye be not deceived: for many shall come in my name, saying, I am Christ and the time draweth near: go ye not therefor after them. ⁹But when ye shall hear of wars and commotions, be not terrified: for these things must first come to pass; but the end is not by and by.¹⁰Then said he unto them, Nation shall rise against nation, and kingdom against kingdom: ¹¹And great earthquakes shall be in diverse places, and famines, and pestilences: and fearful sights and great signs shall there be from heaven. ¹²But before all these things, they shall lay their hands on you, and persecute you, delivering you up to the synagogues, and into prisons, being brought before kings and rulers for my name's sake.*

Luke identifies that Jesus says "…but before all these things…" suggesting that *before* nation rises against nation and kingdom against kingdom, Jesus followers will be persecuted. So, when we compare all three, can we determine what "then" means?

26

Matthew writes,

*⁸All these are the beginning of sorrows. ⁹Then shall they deliver you up to be afflicted....*

Mark states,

*⁸For nation shall rise against nation, and kingdom against kingdom: and there shall be earthquakes in diverse places, and there shall be famines and troubles: these are the beginnings of sorrows. ⁹But take heed to yourselves: for they shall deliver you up to councils....*

And Luke explains,

*¹⁰...Nation shall rise against nation, and kingdom against kingdom: ¹¹And great earthquakes shall be in diverse places, and famines, and pestilences: and fearful sights and great signs shall there be from heaven. ¹²But before¹⁰ all these things, they shall lay their hands on you, and persecute you....*

What is the common "then" between all three?  The word "then" appears to share one common meaning between all three accounts: the time after the deception begins but before physical activities between nations and in the heavens commence. Further, the persecution doesn't read as a one-time event where it happens and then is over; it reads like persecution begins and continues for an extended period. It is interesting that, in Luke 21, the persecution of Jesus-

---

[10] πρό pronounced as pro (Strongs G4253).  Sometimes the word meta is used in Greek, which can mean "with" as in "with the time of sorrows" however, the word Luke uses is pro which has a definite meaning of "before."

followers begins before any *critical* cataclysmic activities begin to unfold: the persecution appears to start in the beginning stages of *the beginnings of sorrows*, with light birth pangs. As we will see, this appears to agree with the Revelation.

---

**Prophecy Watch**: Before cataclysmic events begin, Jesus' followers will be attacked and persecuted. This begins the time of sorrows and continues through the end.

---

So how did we get stuck on the word "then"? It's because as we were reading Mt 24, we landed on verse nine that reads:

> *⁹Then shall they deliver you up to be afflicted and shall kill you: and ye shall be hated of all nations for my name's sake.*

Our focus on "then" is to identify when "then" happens, and we can conclude "then" is at the very beginning of the time of sorrows. Jesus and Paul both tell us not to be deceived. Paul clarifies that it's the love of the truth that will keep us from deception, and before all of this, both Jesus and Paul start off with "be not deceived."

I think it's noteworthy that we are being told not to be deceived in a time of trial and persecution; a time when we will want to see Jesus come for the elect of God; a time when we will likely feel we deserve to be saved from the trials we are in, after all we are the elect, right? It is likely for these reasons that Jesus so specifically states His concerns. He warns us from the beginning as noted in Matthew 24:4-5:

> *⁴Take heed that no man deceive you. ⁵For many shall come in my name, saying: I am Christ; and shall deceive many.*

We will *want* Jesus to come; we will be *looking* for Him to come, but He won't come when we expect Him. Luke even captures Jesus' saying this in his account. Recall this verse in Luke 21:8?

*⁸And he said, Take heed that ye be not deceived....*

Before we keep reading, I want to underscore Jesus' warning: look out so that you are not led astray, not deceived, that you don't believe something that is not true. Now, let's continue reading:

*⁸And he said, Take heed that ye be not deceived: for many shall come in my name, saying, I am Christ; and the time draweth near: go ye not therefor after them.*

Luke captures Jesus as specifically warning the hearers of His words not to be deceived *because* many will come in His name saying they are Christ; and many will come in His name saying

*⁸...the time draweth near.*

Jesus warns us that many will come saying "the time of Jesus' return is near!" Let's be certain we understand: Jesus *is* coming! That is beyond dispute. There is a time that people will say "Jesus could come at any moment!" and they will be right; but Jesus says, before the real time comes for His return, there will be a big push where people will say "Jesus is coming" and it will seem believable: don't believe the hype because it's not real. Jesus warns us that there will be a time before His actual return where people will falsely proclaim that His return is close but when there are events yet needing fulfilled. A quick note on this understanding: Jesus does not appear to say that all those declaring His mis-timed return are intentionally trying to deceive people with malice; only that they are deceiving people because their words that are inaccurate.

---

**Be Not Deceived:** And he said, Take heed that ye be not deceived: for many shall come in my name, saying, I am Christ; and the time draweth near: go ye not therefor after them. – Lk 21:8

---

And this one:

---

**Be Not Deceived**: [4]And Jesus answered and said unto them, Take heed that no man deceive you [5]For many shall come in my name, saying, I am Christ; and shall deceive many. – Mt 24:4-5

---

Write these down and commit them to memory and critically ask yourself: "How will I know if I'm being deceived?" Spoiler alert: the answer is not "I just will." None of us knows if we are being deceived: that is the definition of deception.

## Affliction of Jesus' Followers (Mt 24:9-14)

Now that we understand the end-times period launches with "the beginning of sorrows" also known as "the beginning of birth pangs" and that this same timeframe begins the persecution of the elect, let's continue into Matthew 24 and see what happens next. Let's revisit verses eight and nine so we can advance into verse ten.

*<sup>8</sup>All these are the beginning of sorrows. <sup>9</sup>Then shall they deliver you up to be afflicted[11], and shall kill you: and ye shall be hated of all nations for my names' sake. <sup>10</sup>And then shall many be offended, and shall betray one another, and shall hate one another.*

Jesus tells us about the beginning of sorrows in verse eight and tells us that His followers will face the beginning of affliction and will see each other killed, starting at the beginning of sorrows. During this same time, followers of Jesus will be hated "of all[12] nations" (v. 9). Note that this doesn't say, "hated only by Islamic nations" or "hated only by Communist nations." Jesus used the word "all" here. Why would Jesus followers be hated by all nations? And what about Jesus' words that say

*<sup>10</sup>...then shall many be offended, and shall betray one another, and shall hate one another.*

The Greek word for offended[13] is the word skandalizō. This word looks much like the word scandalize in English, doesn't it? The Greek word means to put a stumbling block in front of a person, or to put an impediment in front of them to cause them to stumble and fall; to cause a person to distrust; to cause to fall away. When Jesus says, "...then shall many be offended" He is saying that people will have a stumbling block placed in front of them that causes them to distrust another person and from the vantage point of that

---

[11] The word *afflicted* here is the same Greek word as *tribulation* in Mt 24:21, it is the word θλῖψις pronounced thlip'-sis (Strongs G2347).

[12] πᾶς pronounced as pas (Strongs G3956) . This can mean: all, every, all men, whosoever, everyone, whether individually, corporately or as a representation of every group.

[13] σκανδαλίζω pronounced as skan-dal-id'-zo (Strongs G4624).

stumbling block, they will betray them. Out of deception and fear these people will fall prey to a scandalous attempt of the enemy and they will betray those they love. This again is an interesting part of what must exist behind the Scripture. Scripture does not answer for us the following questions: What is so bad that people would betray one another? What is so bad that they would be offended? At what are they offended? To whom or what are they betraying one another? What are the rules for betrayal? Luke 21:16 adds to this prophecy when Luke records:

> *16And ye shall be betrayed both by parents, and bretheren, and kinsfolk, and friends; and some of you shall they cause to be put to death.*

Luke points out it is parents betraying you, brethren betraying you, cousins, nieces, nephews and friends betraying you; some to the point of death! What scandal would cause people to betray one another knowing that they will be killing their own family members and friends? What scandal would cause people to protect their selves with such unfeeling action? Let's keep reading and see if we can make some patterns out of the rest of Jesus' words.

> *11And many false prophets shall rise, and shall deceive many. 12And because iniquity shall abound, the love of many shall wax cold. 13but he that shall endure unto the end, the same shall be saved.*

During the time that Jesus followers are hated by every nation, false prophets will rise and deceive many. A prophet tells people what God is saying, a prophet directs people to sound doctrine, a prophet offers direction and correction to others. During the time that the world hates Jesus' followers, some identifying as the voice of God on earth will lead others away from sound doctrine, toward false correction and will say what God is *not* saying. Also, "iniquity will abound" during this time. Interestingly, the word "iniquity[14]" here is a word which can mean "without law" or "in absence of it." The idea in this verse is lawlessness: "It doesn't apply to me! I can do what I want with whom I want when I want and there is nothing wrong with anything if I decide it is that way!"

Jesus says that in the last days before His return, this mindset of lawlessness, being without boundaries and above rule, will *abound* and because it is pervasive, the love of many will grow cold as if a person were blowing over the top of hot tea or cooling down by evaporation[15]. My interpretation of Jesus words is:

*People will become so focused on their own self-motivated definition, they will make themselves god and decide what is right and wrong in their own eyes—no absolutes—only what is desirable without concern for consequences in God's eyes; they will cast away a love of the truth and in their deception, absence of law will blow over their love and cause evaporation, their love will evaporate, grow cold and become more difficult to sense: love and truth will lose their meaning.*

Jesus then ends this part of Matthew 24 by saying:

*[13]But he that shall endure to the end, the same shall be saved. [14]And this gospel of the kingdom shall be*

---

[14] ἀνομία pronounced as an-om-ee'-ah (Strongs G458)
[15] ψύχω pronounced psoo'-kho (Strongs G5594)

*preached in all the world for a witness unto all nations; and then shall the end come.*

Jesus completes this section of thought by telling us there is hope, there is an ability to endure to the end of the time of sorrows and if we do, we will be saved. Now, don't misinterpret that verse to mean that *only* those who make it to the end of sorrows are saved: the end of sorrows means the elect of that time not giving up, not loving their lives, not giving in to the world or to satan during that time: it means persevering to the point of death or deliverance, whichever happens first. The word *endure* means to remain behind, not to recede or flee, to hold fast to one's faith in Jesus[16]. Those who endure shall be saved. I think it's interesting that Jesus is telling the disciples and those in the end times "he that endures…shall be saved." Jesus isn't telling his followers they won't need to worry about the end-times events; Jesus speaks into history and tells the elect to persevere.

## What Does John Say?

We've looked at corresponding parts of Matthew, Mark and Luke that all discuss these end-times events, but what about John's gospel? Interestingly, John doesn't talk about the end-times events the same way the other gospel writers do, but I do find it interesting that in the place of John's gospel, where he may have discussed the end times, he records a prayer of Jesus instead. Here is what John 17:14-21 captures:

> *[14]I have given them* [the disciples] *thy word; and the world hath hated them, because they are not of the world, even as I am not of the world. [15]I pray not that*

---

[16] ὑπομένω pronounced hoop-om-en'-o (Strongs G5278)

*thou shouldest take them out of the world, but that thou shouldest keep them from the evil. <sup>16</sup>They are not of the world, even as I am not of the world. <sup>17</sup>Sanctify them through thy truth: thy word is truth. <sup>18</sup>As thou hast sent me into the world, even so have I also sent them into the world. <sup>19</sup>And for their sakes I sanctify myself, that they also might be sanctified through the truth. <sup>20</sup>Neither pray I for these alone, but for them also which shall believe on me through their word; <sup>21</sup>That they all may be one; as thou, Father, [art] in me, and I in thee, that they also may be one in us: that the world may believe that thou hast sent me.*

When Jesus prays to His Father, do you believe He is praying according to God's perfect will?  Does Jesus get whatever He asks for from his Father?  Is there ever a time in Scripture when Jesus prays and doesn't receive what He asks from God?  If there was ever a person who knew how to pray and what to pray for, Jesus would be the one.  Look at what Jesus asks from His Father:

*<sup>15</sup>I pray not that thou shouldest take them out of the world, but that thou shouldest keep them from the evil"*

and just before that He says

*<sup>14</sup>I have given them thy word; and the world hated them, because they are not of the world, even as I am not of the world.*

Do you see the parallels between in John and Matthew, Mark and Luke?  The focus for Jesus-followers is persevering, not quitting, not giving up, not leaving, even when we are hated by the world. Jesus literally prays in John 17:15,20 asking God for something specific for every one of His disciples for all time:

> *15I pray not that thou shouldest take them out of the world, but that thou shouldest keep them from the evil... 20Neither pray I for these alone, but for them also which shall believe on me through their word;*

Does that sound to you like Jesus is asking God to take His followers out before the evil comes? To believe that Jesus wants the elect off the earth before evil comes, one must fully ignore or disregard these words of Jesus.

To be clear, I would love to see Jesus take the elect from the earth early in the end-times events, but I see exactly the opposite in Scripture. We cannot allow our own desires to interpret Scripture, we must change our perceptions to what Scripture declares. We need to write this Scripture down and get it in our hearts because Jesus is the same yesterday, today and forever (Heb 13:8)—if He didn't want us taken out of the world when he walked the earth, He doesn't want us taken out now and He won't want us taken out in the end times.

---

**Jesus Wants Us in the World** – I pray not that thou shouldest take them out of the world, but that thou shouldest keep them from the evil. – John 17:15

---

One last underscore on John 17 before we move on. This prayer of Jesus is just as much for the end-times church as it is for the church in AD30. And you know what else, it's because He wants His church to be one in unity and purpose and pursuit of God. Jesus knows that trials and difficulties *fuse* the elect together with each other and with Him; He knows trials bring focus. Jesus says He wants us to be one, just as He and the Father are one. There is something catalytic about the trying of our faith and Jesus doesn't want us to miss it.

## Pulling It Together (Mt 24:1-14)

In Matthew 24:1-14, Jesus begins by telling the disciples the temple will be destroyed, that not one stone will be left on another (v. 2). The disciples are concerned and ask three questions in response: 1) When shall these things [the temple's destruction] be? 2) What shall be the sign of thy coming? and 3) [What shall be the sign] of the end of the world? Jesus doesn't immediately answer their questions, but begins by laying the most important foundation for the last days and His appearing when He says "…take heed that no man deceive you" (v. 4).

Then Jesus explains a sequence of events which result in the following: we will hear of wars and rumors of wars and about the same time we start to hear these rumors, followers of Jesus will experience increased affliction: Jesus' followers will be delivered to others for punishment merely because they are Jesus' followers for enforcement reasons not explained—they will be hated by the world because Jesus was hated by the world; they will be afflicted and punished; betrayed by parents, siblings, cousins, friends and all these people will do so knowing those they betray could be killed. Even with all this, Jesus says the end is not yet. This isn't the Americanized idea of hate and betrayal where people throw pop bottles and bricks at one another and where the police come out with fire hoses to disburse the crowds. This is true hate and true betrayal to the depth of a human soul.

At the same time of this increased hatred of Jesus and His followers, nation will rise against nation in war and inside nations, kingdoms will battle each other. These times are the beginning of birth pangs and will grow closer together as they become more painful and last longer between rests. Iniquity and lawlessness increase at that time, not merely civil unrest, but individuals focusing on their selves and refusing to accept the fact that eternal consequences exist for actions. This lawlessness will work like a wind blowing across the love of each individual, evaporating it and cooling it. Those who do not keep their love warm will experience it growing cold—it's a basic law of spiritual thermodynamics because heat always dissipates in cold.

As the birth pangs occur, Scripture suggests the days will look like the following example: we will see a trial of intensity level one followed by a resting period where many will think "I'm glad *that* is over." But then, perhaps another trial of intensity level one will follow, and that trial will be tagged by another rest. Again, those who do not know the truth and that for which to watch will express relief and consider the pattern of trial and rest as a coincidence. Those who know how to watch will begin identifying and speaking often of these patterns of trial, rest, more intense trial, shorter rest, more intense trial, shorter rest. This process will repeat as the trials increase in intensity, and the time between trials becomes less. People will begin to tire, and their hope will be challenged. Those who understand Scripture will turn their gaze upward to find hope in Jesus alone, those individuals not looking to Jesus will become more and more hardened.

In the midst of all this, many Jesus followers who do not yet understand but who have an honest love for God may look for meaning, asking God "why" and perhaps even questioning what they know to be true, maybe wondering why they are here on earth during the time of these occurrences, wondering why they are experiencing these difficulties when they've been told by teachers in their life that they would be gone before anything evil happened; and it is at this point that Jesus' words will take on more weight "see that no man deceive you" and "he that endures to the end shall be saved."

In this vacuum, when times are difficult, the Christian world will then see individuals arise and exclaim they are speaking for God. Some of these may be well-meaning, thinking they are encouraging the elect while others are purposefully being used of satan to lead people away from their faith. In both cases, they are false and only those who are watching for Scripture-defined events and comparing the words of these teachers against Scripture will know if it is truly God speaking. These people will come authoritatively declaring they know God's voice and His plans, and they will deceive many. Some will possibly tell Jesus' followers and others that they must conform to the world systems to avoid punishment while others will continue trying to convince people that they will leave soon so they don't need to do anything but "look up for your redemption draweth nigh." In both cases, people will listen to the deception and make decisions that will cost them their life.

Attempting to cope on their own, instead of turning to Jesus for their focus, strength and truth, people will become even more lawless and depend on their own definition of truth, relying on the normal as truth instead of the truth itself.

In this time of lawlessness, rules will be established, and scandal promoted, that will put great pressure on individuals. They will embrace the scandal or risk being punished or possibly executed their selves. In this confusion and pressure, perhaps out of self-preservation, people will choose to love themselves rather than the truth and this will lead to more and more people betraying each other, some knowingly betrayed to death. Those who are going through this great pressure and who love God will need to endure this time to make it through, and if they persevere without giving up on their faith, Jesus says "the same shall be saved" (v. 13).

That, my friends, is what I perceive Matthew 24:1-14 to discuss. Now remember, this is the beginning of the end – the time of sorrows – the time of birth pangs. Unfortunately, it gets more intense as we continue reading Jesus' words. At this point, we aren't even in the Great Tribulation period yet: that is still ahead! So, here is one parting thought as we leave Mt 24:1-14: Jesus is explaining the beginning of the end; have you seen the catching away of Jesus' elect yet? On the contrary, what we see is that through the gospels, Jesus is trying to encourage His followers not to give up, not to give in, to be strengthened and to experience His indwelling presence just as His Father is living inside of Him. Let's keep watching for the gathering of the elect as we study. Jesus does reference it in His teaching. Is your interest piqued? Wait till Matthew 24:15!

# The Abomination of Desolation

In Mt 24:1-14, Jesus begins to answer three questions: 1) When shall these things [the temple's destruction] be? 2) What shall be the sign of thy coming? and 3) [What shall be the sign] of the end of the world? Jesus answers seemingly off topic when He starts with the phrase, "Take heed that no man deceive you" (Mt 24:4). Jesus then lays down a timeline that you can re-read at the end of the previous chapter, but which, in summary, states: deceivers will come, you will be hated of all nations, you will hear of wars and some of you put to death, real wars will begin, the events will increase pressure on humankind, people will begin betraying each other, difficulties will increase, and do not give up! In Mt 24:14 Jesus ends His initial thoughts with these words:

> *14And this gospel of the kingdom shall be preached in all the world for a witness unto all nations; and then shall the end come.*

Jesus lays out the beginning of the end times, also known as the time of sorrows and the time of birth pangs, and then He brings it to an abrupt end in verse 14. You will understand by the end of this study, if you don't already, that there is *much more* that happens in the end times that is not covered in detail in Mt 24:1-14! But, to understand verse 15, we must understand that Jesus punctuated His thoughts. He said in essence, "Hey…everything I just said in verses 1-14? Just understand it is ongoing and there's more I'm not covering right now, but just know—before the end comes, the gospel of the kingdom of God will go fully into all the earth. The end won't happen until the gospel is preached everywhere! When you see that happen, then you will know for certain: the end is nearly here."

This is very important, because without understanding the timing of Mt 24:1-14, we cannot understand the timing of Mt 24:15. Jesus continues teaching in verse 15 by stating:

*15When ye therefore shall see the abomination of desolation, spoken of by Daniel the prophet, stand in the holy place, (whoso readeth, let him understand)....*

Jesus goes from "…and then shall the end come" to "when ye therefore shall see the abomination of desolation…." How did we get from the end of the world to seeing the abomination? If we just hit the end of the world, wouldn't that suggest there is nothing more that can happen? We will see these intertwining Scriptures all through our study, and we would do well to recognize this pattern now. Over and again, we will see a series of events that start somewhere, and end somewhere, immediately followed by an insertion that lands somewhere during what we just read.

I offered an example earlier about my driving from Oklahoma City to Dallas and making phone calls but let me offer one or two more examples to further illustrate how this works.

Here is an example in story form. I'll write it to you as a letter since that's pretty much what the Bible is.

*Dear You,*

*There is a conference in Paris, and I want to attend. I have so much to do. I need to get a dog sitter, my passport, and some new luggage. The conference will last a week and at the end of the week, I'll fly home and then probably go straight to bed, because I fully expect to be exhausted! I really can't wait to go, but I know I'll be very glad to be home when I'm done!*

Now, if I were to leave the story at that point, we don't yet have the example Jesus' words present: we only have the story, but no actionable, backward-facing insertion point. The pattern of this fictional story is, for all intents, just like Mt 24:1-14: it is a complete account with a beginning and a defined end. Now, let me re-write the story and include the backward facing point that inserts detail into the story line, even though it is recorded at the *end* of the storyline. Here we go:

*Dear You,*

*There is a conference in Paris, and I want to attend. I have so much to do. I need to get a dog sitter, my passport, and some new luggage. The conference will last a week and at the end of the week, I'll fly home and then probably go straight to bed, because I fully expect to be exhausted! I really can't wait to go, but I know I'll be very glad to be home when I'm done! One thing I can't wait to do is experience the Champs-Élysées: I hear it is beautiful!*

This is a good example of the entire storyline with an insertion of color after the fact. I told you: there is a conference in Paris; I have much to do; it will last a week; I plan to be exhausted; when I come home, I'm going straight to bed; but, while I'm there, I plan to visit a famous tourist site.

Let me do another shorter example to further illustrate this communication technique.

*Jesus was born the human Son of God; Jesus lived a sinless life; Jesus died on the cross for your sins; Jesus was resurrected from the dead in a new body; Jesus will come again[4]; and when all history is coming to an end, as His final action[B], Jesus will judge the nations of the world and return all power and dominion to God His Father. Even though mankind will hate Jesus and want to destroy him with immeasurable force, that will not stop Jesus from fulfilling His mission! He will come and rule with a rod of iron for 1,000 years before the end occurs.*

Here is another example: I give the entirety of Jesus' life and explain He will be the ultimate Authority, ultimate Judge and ultimate Power. Then, I insert color into the storyline, that belongs somewhere after the midpoint of the story, by saying that even though people will hate Him, it

44

will not stop Him from reaching His goal. In the story above, I marked the in and out points with an A and B so you can see where my insertion should go. You should conclude that this detail fits somewhere at or after the A and at or before the B.

Why does this type of writing happen you might wonder? I honestly think it is one of a few possibilities, perhaps all of them. First, it seems to support your ability to focus on the meaning of the account without getting dragged down in details that really need explained in and of their selves. Using this technique, I can walk you through the entire account of some historic or future series, and help you understand the full chain of events. Then, once you get the overall sequence, I can come back and fill in gaps with more details, each of which may be their own account and chain of events.

Another possibility to consider is if someone were handwriting you a letter in ink, and that person had no way to erase and insert details, he or she would be forced to use this technique or else re-write one or more pages of the letter. The Scriptures were all hand-written: there was no way to insert details. It may be that in some cases, the insertion of details after the account's conclusion is because there was no other way for the writer to effectively expound the additional detailed thoughts.

In either or both cases, the outcome is the same: information introduced later in the account needs inserted somewhere in the previous event chain, and we must try and discern where it fits. Because this understanding is extremely important, let me offer one more example to drive this home:

*The war against Nazi Germany was a global phenomenon. Were it not for the battle of the Bulge, the battle of Berlin and the battle of Midway, the world would likely look much different.*

In this example, the next words I would likely write would be ones to interact in detail with the battle of Midway, then to unpack the battle of Berlin and finally to unpack the battle of the Bulge: all in appropriate detail. Were I to have written the detail of all three of those wars in the above introductory paragraph, the outcome would have been chapters of writing and you would have completely missed the fact I was attempting to make before moving forward: that these three battles appear key to the ultimate defense that stopped World War II. The details of these battles are very important, but no less important is the fact that the three of them were strategic keys to the outcome. Are you understanding? **There are times where the author or communicator wants you to understand the event sequence without the details, because the sequence itself is valuable as are the details that happen inside it.**

## Abomination of Desolation (Mt 24:15)

The abomination of desolation is the first defining point that Jesus offers in His discourse about the end-times events. When I say "defining point" I specifically mean that there is enough detail on this observation that we will know specifically when it happens, give or take a few minutes or hours of its occurrence. This is different from "wars and rumors of wars" which have happened for millennia. It is hard to know when the "wars and rumors of wars" Jesus references will begin, but the abomination of desolation is very specific with lots of detail: this one event we can target, identify and use as a pivotal time for things that happened before and after. No doubt, this is why Jesus specifically references it. Of the three gospels covering end-times events (Matthew, Mark and Luke), only Matthew and Mark capture Jesus words about the "abomination of desolation." Let's read them back-to-back. First Mt 24:15-16:

> *15When ye therefore shall see the abomination of desolation, spoken of by Daniel the prophet, stand in the holy place, (whoso readeth, let him understand:) 16then let them which be in Judea flee into the mountains....*

and now Mark 13:14:

> *14But when ye shall see the abomination of desolation, spoken of by Daniel the prophet, standing where it ought not, (let him that readeth understand,) then let them that be in Judea flee to the mountains....*

In both occurrences, the abomination of desolation is visible; both note it's spoken of by Daniel the prophet; both tell people in Judea to flee to the mountains. One difference between the two gospels is that Matthew states the abomination of desolation will "...stand in the holy place..." while Mark states the abomination of desolation will be seen "...standing where it ought not...." The point of the parallelism between the two scriptures is that sometime in the days known as the beginnings of sorrows or the beginnings of birth pangs, before the world comes to an end, an entity known as "the abomination of desolation" will be visible and it will be identified as standing in "the holy place" (Mt 24:15) "where it ought not" (Mk 13:14). We are further told, in plain terms: Hey! If you don't know the value and consequence of the abomination of desolation as it was defined by Daniel the prophet, you need to stop what you're doing and go figure it out, because this is very important and if you gloss over it, you're cheating yourself out of truth— and this is truth you need!

What is this "abomination of desolation" that both Matthew and Mark discuss? And what does Daniel have to do with understanding it? To answer these questions, we need to jump over to the book of Daniel and see what the prophet said about it.

*Daniel Identifies the Abomination (Dan 11:31)*

In Daniel 11:31, we read the following prophecy:

> *31And arms shall stand on his part, and they shall pollute the sanctuary of strength, and shall take away the daily sacrifice, and they shall place the abomination that maketh desolate.*

Here, we read Daniel's words directly: some of the words that Jesus referenced. Daniel 11 is the longest prophecy in the entirety of Scripture. Nearly the entire chapter of Daniel 11 is one long prophecy: all 45 verses of it. The fascinating thing about Daniel 11 is that it represents the history leading up to the final world ruler before Jesus, the one we will identify in the book of the Revelation as "the beast" and that you've seen me reference as the beast-man[17] in earlier pages.

---

[17] I use the term beast-man because as we will later learn, the beast can be any of five different entities, all of which require context to discern. The beast can be: the angel abaddon also known as appollyon from the bottomless pit, it can be the man who is the end-times world ruler, it can be the man who is the religious ruler working under the

This man who becomes known as *the beast* is a very twisted, demonic, genius who is extremely skilled at manipulating and maneuvering on the global stage. Here in Daniel 11:31, we see that military force does a few things for this beast-man:

- First, they stand on his part: a military entity made up of soldiers, likely from inside and outside Israel, who forsake the holy covenant[18], are opposed to Israel's direction and who take a position to represent the beast-man.

- Second, they "pollute the sanctuary of strength" suggesting that they either create a place that is unholy, or they make a holy place unholy (discussed later).

- Third, they take away the "daily *sacrifice.*" I put the word *sacrifice* in italics because the word *sacrifice* is not in the original Hebrew which only uses the word tamid (תָּמִיד) and this is very important. The word means "continuity" and refers to the sacrificial practices of the Jews but is much larger than merely a sacrifice or even multiple sacrifices – it is more the daily, continuous experience of worship that it represents. Set this aside and we'll return to it later.

---

beast-man, it can be a world political system and it can be a world financial system. We will discuss these in detail later.

[18] The holy covenant is defined for us in the gospel of Luke 1:72-75, "72To perform the mercy [promised] to our fathers, and to remember his holy covenant; 73The oath which he sware to our father Abraham, 74That he would grant unto us, that we being delivered out of the hand of our enemies might serve him without fear, 75In holiness and righteousness before him, all the days of our life" – Lk 1:72-75.

For now, just realize that the military stops this from happening.

- Fourth and finally, the military force places the "abomination that maketh desolate" in this place, which appears to be what defiles the place and makes it an abomination.

It is this fourth point that drives home how the term *abomination of desolation* gets its name. It is the amalgam of the pieces that creates the definition and in essence can be explained as: the image of a false god placed in a location that should be for the pure worship of God Almighty ("the abomination") as a byproduct "of" the destruction ("desolation") being produced by military force, thus "abomination of desolation."

These are the events Jesus is referencing as recorded in Mt 24:15 and Mk 13:14. We will dive into Daniel's understanding of the final beast-man later, but for now, just realize the following:

---

**The abomination of desolation** references an image, idol or piece of technology that represents the beast-man, is able to speak at the hands of the beast-man and is established publicly by military force in a location that is defiling and where it should not be.

---

Jesus says that the people of the last days will see this happen, and that this event is *definitive!* Again, remember, Jesus is saying this; Jesus is telling us how pivotal this point is to our understanding. Now, before we go too far into what happens next, what does Luke write about this? As I said before, Luke doesn't talk about the abomination of desolation, yet Luke's gospel is one of the three that covers named end-times events, so what does Luke write?

In Luke 21:20-22 we have the account of what he gathered. Remember, Luke was not one of the 12 apostles. Luke watched from the outside. Whether Luke was alive when Jesus was or not, we know that he was close to the origin of the events themselves—if not there directly, immediately interacting with those who were eyewitnesses from the beginning[19]. Luke takes on the responsibility of writing Jesus' life and teaching and in his gospel, he records the following:

> [20]*And when ye shall see Jerusalem compassed with armies, then know that the desolation thereof is nigh.* [21]*Then let them which are in Judea flee to the mountains; and let them which are in the midst of it depart out; and let not them that are in the countries enter thereinto.* [22]*For these be the days of vengeance, that all things which are written may be fulfilled.*

Luke is the only one of the three that identifies military involvement, and he still used the word *desolation* but not in association with an abominable thing being placed anywhere. He also doesn't tell the reader to make certain to understand. In the other two gospels, Matthew and Mark neglect to discuss the military presence but do discuss the abominable thing being placed; Luke omits the abominable thing being placed but discusses the military presence.

---

[19] Luke 1:2 states he interacted with those who saw firsthand.

It's when we look at all three gospels combined that we can put together the understanding Jesus taught and that the book of Daniel also captures:

1. there will be military force;
2. they will compass Jerusalem;
3. there will be an abominable thing placed in the holy place where it should not be;
4. all these reference Daniel's prophecy; and,
5. when you see this Daniel prophetic event, you need to take immediate action!

Interestingly, Luke catches Jesus' words driving home that the time of the great tribulation period are the "days of vengeance, that all things which are written may be fulfilled." In these days, the culmination of every remaining Scripture ever written will be initiated[20]: we are indeed reaching the end of history as we know it and the remainder of the full plan of God for mankind will be set in motion.

## The Days of the Gentiles

You may be wondering what the phrase "the days of the gentiles" means. This was a bit difficult to find and as best I can derive from Scripture, it seems the days of the gentiles began at or before the fall of the temple in AD70 and continue to this day. These days will continue until Jesus returns to physically rule over the earth. It appears *the days of the gentiles* include the fact that:

---

[20] This is revealed to John in the revelation and happens at the 7th seal found in Rev 10:7: "7But in the days of the voice of the seventh angel, when he shall begin to sound, the mystery of God should be finished, as he hath declared to his servants the prophets."

- Jerusalem is compassed with armies – this likely agrees with and happens when the abomination of desolation is set up and is referenced in Dan 11:30-31;
- there is great distress in the land of Israel;
- there is wrath[21] (executed judgment) upon the people;
- the people of Israel fall by the edge of the sword;
- the people of Israel are led away captive into all nations;
- Jerusalem is trodden down under the gentiles.

To be certain, I understand that some or all these points may be perceived by some as having already happened, leaving only the last point as a future event. This possibility only underscores how far into the days of the gentiles we may be. As we will see when our journey takes us through the topic of *The Day of the Lord*, these points all gain much more understanding as we observe how the gentiles are a thorn in the flesh of Israel all through the end times.

It seems most believable to me that we can understand "gentiles" to mean: members of Islam or any other individual who does not recognize Israel's inheritance over the land of Israel and the city of Jerusalem making the days of the gentiles not just a time where gentiles are being saved by Jesus, but where non-Jews with unbiblical intent force their presence against the Jewish people as we see now between Islam, Israel and the argument over the temple

---

[21] ὀργή pronounced as or-gay (Strongs G3709) and which means the executed wrath of God. This is different than the wrath included in the seven vials of the Revelation, which is the word θυμός pronounced as thoo-mos' (Strongs G2372) which represents God's hot displeasure toward something and His hot breath toward something.

mount in Jerusalem. And for the record, Scripture seems fairly clear to me that Jerusalem will *always* be in conflict until Jesus returns to rule the earth. Whenever peace exists in Jerusalem, it seems from Scripture that it will always be short-lived until Jesus physical return; and while the days of the gentiles appear to have begun nearly 2,000 years ago, it is only amped up and fueled by the abomination of desolation being established in the holy place of Jerusalem.

## The Holy Place Defined

What I'm about to write, I realize may garner some push-back, and that's okay. Healthy interaction is what it takes to find truth in many cases. After 1,400+ hours of research, I do not believe the term "holy place" as referenced by Jesus must be the third fully-constructed temple structure itself, but that it can be any place geographically defined as "holy" by the Jewish leaders. Let me explain why. Israel is currently apostate in many ways. When you watch Israeli news, follow the interactions of the Jewish religious rulers, review information about the temple mount and follow current Jewish teaching, the Jewish people are primed for a messiah, but not yet for Jesus as messiah. The atmosphere for the antichrist to appear is electric.

However, in all this confusion, the preparations for temple worship are done. As I write these words in 2022, Israel has already created the garb for the priests, the elements of sacrifice, the altar for sacrifice, the altar of incense and myriad other items. The men to serve as priests and Levites have been identified. They have "practiced" the Passover sacrifice, the daily tamid sacrifice and the Rosh Hashanah sacrifice. They have even "practiced" the creation of the holy anointing oil for the temple and have "practiced" anointing the high priest as of December 6,

2021.  Be certain to understand, Scripture does not allow for the Jews to practice creating the holy anointing oil or to practice anointing a high priest.  To state these events are "practice" is, in my opinion, only a way to keep political tension from exploding over their worship practices.

We will discuss why these elements are so important when we arrive in Daniel, however, let me explain here why these play into my perception of the Holy Place and the abomination of desolation.  The word tamid[22] is used to reference the daily sacrifice that happened in Israel in the morning and evening, and it also references the continuous acts of Jewish worship.  When the term tamid was first used, it was at the Exodus of Israel from Egypt and not in the temple: it predates the temple.

Next, the term "holy place" in Mt 24:15 is made up of two Greek words: holy meaning "set apart" and place[23] meaning "any marked off space."  The Greek translation suggests it can be any marked space that is considered holy. This phrase references the prophecy in Daniel 11:31 where the term "sanctuary of strength" is used to identify the location for the abomination of desolation.  This phrase *sanctuary of strength* is very odd, because this term never appears anywhere else in the Bible and is never used to identify the temple or tabernacle used when the Jews first exited Egypt.  The Hebrew word *sanctuary*[24] has been used as a reference to things consecrated as well as the early tabernacle in the wilderness and the temple itself.  It can

---

[22] תָּמִיד pronounced taw-meed' (Strongs H8548) means: continuity, perpetuity, to stretch, continually, continuously.  It never specifically references an animal sacrifice.

[23] τόπος pronounced top'-os (Strongs G5117).

[24] מִקְדָּשׁ pronounced mik-dawsh' (Strongs H4720)

mean an asylum and it even references holy places declared to be so by a king of Israel. The modifier word of *strength*[25] carries the definition of safety, protection, stronghold and refuge—it is a fortified place. Stating that the term *sanctuary of strength* means the Jewish Temple doesn't fit and never did because the Jewish temple was never a stronghold. However, when you consider the Roman fortress of Antonia exists at the temple mount, I begin to wonder if it will play a part in this definition.

What I'm about to write is 100% my opinion. My intent is not to offend any Jewish readers and is admittedly coming from a systems analyst with an eye on international events and not a Jewish scholar. From that vantage point, I am not saying I am right, but I am watching to see if the following thoughts, or something close to these thoughts, happen.

I believe what we are told here is that the *holy place* Jesus spoke of that is called *the sanctuary of strength* by Daniel, will be a physical area that is allocated and approved by the Jewish religious and political leadership that will reside on the Temple Mount in Israel. I don't believe it needs a building or even a tent. It can simply be an area of the temple mount in Jerusalem that is dedicated to the daily practice of Jewish worship. I believe this could even be open air, with painted lines for walls. In essence, it could be a 12' by 12' square on the temple mount where the sacrificial altar may be placed. No building is needed. It appears all that needs to happen for the daily sacrifice to start is for the Jewish leaders to establish this place, erect the altar and begin sacrificing. Doing this would meet the definition of *sanctuary of strength* since it is an area set apart that has

---

[25] מָעוֹז pronounced maw-oze' (Strongs H4581)

geographic relationship to the fortress and because it is declared to be holy by Jewish leadership. When you consider: the daily sacrifice was started before a temple existed; holy places can be defined by Israelite kings; the existing priesthood is ready to begin; and the fortress of Antonia was used to store the priestly elements; I believe the nation of Israel wants the sacrifices so badly that they will find any way they can to begin them, even if it means bending the rules to see it happen. We've already watched the religious rulers bend the rules as we've watched them "practice" the different aspects of worship and I believe this process of bending the rules will continue.

*Why Does This Matter?*

This matters because when the abomination of desolation is established, the daily tamid practice stops, and for it to stop, it must first start. At the writing of this chapter in early 2022, the practice of the daily sacrifice is not yet a regular occurrence. Could the *practice* sacrifices fulfill this Scripture? We will only know in hindsight. For now, however, we are watching for a more regular, daily, priestly worship experience as a necessary prophetic event, and it seems that until the daily tamid practice begins again, we have no need to be concerned about the appearing of the abomination of desolation. Now, to keep this in perspective, I am not aware that Scripture provides a timeframe between the beginning of the tamid practice of the sacrifice and the time it stops at the hands of the beast-man: it could be that it begins on a Tuesday and stops on that Wednesday. However, until it begins, we know the beast-man is not yet ready to be revealed. But! At the point it begins again, the clock is then theoretically ticking in countdown to his appearance.

## What to Do at the Abomination (Mt 24:16-22)

How are we to respond when we see the abomination of desolation that Jesus discusses? Mt 24:16-22 gives specifics. As we continue reading, we see Jesus' instructions when the abomination of desolation is seen standing where it should not be:

> *16Then let them which be in Judaea flee into the mountains: 17Let him which is on the housetop not come down to take anything out of his house: 18Neither let him which is in the field return back to take his clothes. 19And woe unto them that are with child, and to them that give suck in those days! 20But pray ye that your flight be not in the winter, neither on the sabbath day: 21For then shall be great tribulation, such as was not since the beginning of the world to this time, no, nor ever shall be. 22And except those days should be shortened, there should no flesh be saved: but for the elect's sake those days shall be shortened.*

Jesus says to those in Judea, when the abomination of desolation is seen, flee to the mountains! Do it immediately and leave your entire livelihood behind – take *nothing!* Don't go home first if you're at work. Pray and ask God not to let this happen on the Sabbath or during the winter! Because the difficulty that lies ahead will be unlike anything humankind has ever experienced. Jesus is emphatic that time is of the essence, and if you are not ready to flee at the moment it happens, you will experience consequences.

## What Scripture Says Without Saying It

There are some key pieces that are inferred but not spoken in these scriptures of Mt 24:14-15; Mk 13:14 and Lk 21:20-21: let's dig them out.

### Communication Networks

First, the phrase in Mt 24 that reads "¹⁶Then let them which be in Judaea flee into the mountains" leads us to believe that Judea will be the hotbed of activity and that staying there will be the worst decision. From this scripture, we know Judea (the eastern part of Israel and the location of Jerusalem) will be heavily affected by this time in prophecy. Both, Luke's and Daniel's accounts suggest this is true as they discuss Jerusalem being compassed by military force. Luke 21:20 records:

> ²⁰*And when ye shall see Jerusalem compassed with armies, then know that the desolation thereof is nigh.*

The next phrases in Matthew 24 states:

> ¹⁷*Let him which is on the housetop not come down to take anything out of his house:* ¹⁸*Neither let him which is in the field return back to take his clothes.*

These verses drive home the speed with which an individual's response must happen, but they equally drive home the speed with which the military force will take hold. These also underscore the point that all plans and decisions to handle this circumstance must be made in advance: I must have a script to follow that I can simply trigger. I cannot make decisions when these events happen. If I try to save anything from my home, if I try to get to my family, if I and my family do *anything* but flee, our consequences will be severe. We must preplan and execute the plan at a moment's notice!

*Now,* something that Scripture doesn't say, but that must exist for Mt 24:16-18 to be possible! How could someone be in the field, be on top of their house or be anywhere in the countryside of Judea, a geographic area that is ~120 miles tall and ~60 miles wide, and where everyone simultaneously becomes aware by visual or mental perception that the abomination of desolation was *just* placed where it ought not be? The only conceivable way this Scripture could be possible in the way Jesus is describing it would be if there existed, at the time of the placement of the abomination of desolation, a communication network that could reach all these places simultaneously and instantaneously. Think about how illogical Jesus' statement would be in any other context without such a network. Without this network, Jesus' words would read something like this illustration:

> *You who are in Judea, when word travels by mouth from person to person and from shopkeeper to shopkeeper, when you receive a letter from your friend, cousin or parent, as soon as you personally hear the news that the abomination of desolation has been set in the place it ought not be, then you must flee to the mountains! When you hear from your milkman, or from your goat keepers or as soon as you read the letter in your hand, don't come down from your rooftop to get anything from your house! Once the cattle feeders have told you this news, leave everything in the field and flee to the mountains!*

It would take weeks or perhaps months for some percentage of individuals to hear the news, much less

60

everyone in the area that is 7,200 square miles known as Judea; but, in a day where communication is immediate and accessible, delivered to a person on the spot, irrespective of location, at the time or within seconds of an event, this Scripture would be possible and it would be believable for a person anywhere in Judea, whether on a rooftop or in a field, to know with immediacy that something of this extreme nature had happened. Only in a highly connected communications environment will Jesus' words of time sensitivity be possible. This is now.

---

**Prophecy Watch**: Jesus words about how to respond when seeing the abomination of desolation placed where it ought not be could only happen in a generation highly connected to information networks with immediate access to events and notifications.

---

### Lack of Food and Water

Something else that Jesus says without saying it is in Mt 24:19 where we read:

> *[19]And woe unto them that are with child, and to them that give suck in those days!*

Why would Jesus say these words? What is common between women "with child" and women that "give suck"? In both cases, the lives of their children depend wholly on the mother receiving enough water and nourishment to allow for the child in the womb to develop safely and for the nursing baby to receive all the nutrients he or she needs to live a healthy life. In both cases, if the mother is not able to get enough water and nutrients, the baby in the womb or on the breast will likely die from malnutrition. I believe that Jesus is telling us here: when the abomination of desolation becomes visible, water and food will be scarce for a prolonged period or for prolonged periods of time: these will be very difficult times for pregnant and nursing mothers.

---

**Prophecy Watch**: Jesus words of warning to pregnant and nursing mothers could only happen in a situation where they would not have the food and water necessary for their developing babies to receive proper nourishment.

---

*Travel by Foot*

What else does Jesus say without saying it? Consider this verse in Mt. 24:20:

*²⁰But pray ye that your flight be not in the winter, neither on the sabbath day*

Let's start with the sabbath day. Why would it matter if they needed to flee on the sabbath day? The main reason is that humankind is not allowed to work on sabbath days without sinning against God. This means no Jew is to carry anything and it also means a limitation on the number of steps. Perhaps you've read the Scripture and seen the phrase "a sabbath day's journey" in your reading? The Mount of Olives is a "sabbath day's journey" from Jerusalem (Acts 1:12). This, for ease of conversation, means that on any given sabbath day, a person was not allowed to walk more than ~2,000 paces, which was somewhere close to one kilometer or ¾ mile. Having to flee on the sabbath would mean being unprepared, unable to carry anything and would force the Jewish believer to decide between fleeing for their life or breaking the commands of God.

The phrase about not being in winter could refer to the difficulties a person might experience by traveling in snow or cold temperatures if you consider that those being spoken to don't even have time to go down into their houses to get additional clothing. One other thing of interest seems to be that God might intervene if people ask for God to avoid these scenarios. Jesus says "pray" that it won't meet certain circumstances. The fact Jesus said to pray it won't happen seems to suggest God could delay it at the behest of people's prayers.

But I think, in both cases, it seems Jesus is speaking to a future group of individuals who normally could travel any distance they needed on a sabbath, or who would not normally be affected by winter travel. It seems Jesus is speaking to a generation of people who will have to adjust away from their normal lifestyle to adapt to a difficult situation and will need to do it with haste in such a way that they need to process in advance what they will do before it happens *if* it happens on a sabbath or *if* it happens in the winter when their normal resources are not available.

I believe Jesus is talking to a generation who can travel in ways other than foot. You see, on the sabbath, even leading an animal with your family on top of it was considered work. But if you have a vehicle that is motorized, both orthodox and non-orthodox Jews at the writing of this book consider operating a vehicle to save the life of a person as permissible[26]. I believe the recipients of Jesus' words are people in a future generation who could use cars, trucks, etc. to evacuate Judea on the sabbath days, but who will not be able to because roads may be closed or blocked and normal transportation on the sabbath day or in the winter elements will not be possible. **The point being**

---

[26] *Pikuach nefesh* (Heb. פקוח נפש)

**that these people will *need* to evacuate on foot.** Do we know that these words represent an inability to use automobiles? No, we don't; we are however endeavoring to answer the question of why it would matter if the people Jesus references need to flee on a sabbath or in winter, and this is a possible answer. In cases like this one, we make a note of the possibility and we set it aside to see if anything else in our study affirms or rejects the assumption.

Hopefully, you can see why it's important to slow down and consider the thought behind the words. If we merely read these words at face-value and don't stop to ask what needs to exist around these words to make them plausible, we lose the opportunity to see just how futuristic and prophetic these words of Jesus are to those listening, and how no other generation before ours could see them come to pass.

## Those Days

This phrase "those days" in Mt 24:19 is one of the most important pieces of this section of Scripture and arriving at a proper understanding and definition of "those days" is paramount. I would go so far as to say, this one phrase may have the most influence of any other phrase in understanding the timing of the end-day's events.

Let's re-read Mt 24:15-20 so that we see the phrase in context.

> *15When ye therefore shall see the abomination of desolation, spoken of by Daniel the prophet, stand in the holy place, (whoso readeth, let him understand:) 16Then let them which be in Judaea flee into the mountains: 17Let him which is on the housetop not come down to take any thing out of his house:*

*<sup>18</sup>Neither let him which is in the field return back to take his clothes. <sup>19</sup>And woe unto them that are with child, and to them that give suck in those days! <sup>20</sup>But pray ye that your flight be not in the winter, neither on the sabbath day: <sup>21</sup>For then shall be great tribulation, such as was not since the beginning of the world to this time, no, nor ever shall be. <sup>22</sup>And except those days should be shortened, there should no flesh be saved: but for the elect's sake those days shall be shortened.*

What can we gather about the phrase "those days"? First, "those days" begin with the revealing of the abomination of desolation spoken of by Daniel the prophet. We've already discussed how Mt 24:14 was the end of the age, the period ending either at the time of or sometime after Jesus returns to rule the earth for 1,000 years which is known as the millennial reign of Jesus; and then how after the phrase "…and then shall the end come" we went back into the event list to add detail when we arrived at Mt 24:15. The focus has now shifted from the end of the world to the appearing of the abomination of desolation—that is our focus and our topic starting in verse 15. So, "those days" begins with the appearing of the abomination of desolation and continues forward, unraveling day by day over the span of a currently unknown number of days (albeit Daniel and Revelation both give clarity on this).

"Those days" begin with the abomination of desolation and move forward in time according to Jesus; and based on His definition, there is time during "those days" to flee to the mountains of Judea; there is time for pregnant women to suffer difficulties with their unborn children; there is time for nursing mothers to suffer difficulties feeding their infant children; and by the time we reach verses 21-22, we realize that the length of "those days" is long enough, and the circumstances severe enough, that if they had not been stopped early *for the elect's sake*, not a single member of humankind would survive.

It's the last verse that paints a graphic image of how dire these days will be and why pregnant and nursing mothers will suffer so much: these days are unlike any other in the history of humankind—they are worse than anything that has ever happened or ever will happen. It is also this reference to pregnant and nursing mothers, along with the idea of fleeing to the mountains, that helps us understand the period will be over an extended time and not just days or hours.

### How Long is "Those Days"

How long, then, is "those days" according to Jesus? "Those days" start at the revealing of the abomination of desolation and are long enough that pregnant and nursing mothers will suffer with their children and that if they continued at the level of severity Jesus understood, these days would fully destroy humanity. The number of days is not exposed at this point, but we know it must be, at a minimum, long enough to affect malnutrition of women and babies; and long enough to nearly exterminate humanity.

We need to keep track of this expanse that Jesus labeled as "those days" because they create a timeframe to which we will return repeatedly. The days preceding "those days" will quite possibly only be seen and identified in hindsight, meaning, when we get to the abomination of desolation and look back in time, we'll be able to put the pieces together, but going through them while they are happening, these pre-days may not be as easy to identify. I believe this understanding represents why Jesus says in Mt 24:33

> [33]*So likewise ye, when ye shall see all these things, know that it is near, [even] at the doors.*

Jesus tells us, when you see not one, not two, not three of these signs, but when you see all these signs happen then your attention should be aroused. Before moving ahead, we must understand some important aspects of many prophecies.

## Prophecy Road Signs

I perceive that Old Testament prophecies are much like road signs on a highway. As you're driving down the highway at a high velocity, you look in the distance and you see a green sign with silvery-white reflective letters. It's nearly impossible to make out what the sign says at a distance, and yet you have no difficulty seeing that it's a sign. The closer you get to the sign, the more you're able to read the larger letters: big things are discernable from a distance. Then when you finally get close to the sign itself, you're able to read the small text—the details of whatever sort they may be. At that time, with all the understanding you can gather from the sign, you interpret it based on your speed and direction and you begin to answer questions: Is this information necessary? Do I care? Does it affect me? Do I use it to decide? Is this where I exit? How much further do I have to go yet? Given my current velocity, how long will it take to get to the next sign? When will the journey be completed? Are we there yet?

We make sense out of what we see when it becomes perceivable, when we can compare it to previous understandings, and when we ultimately decide if the information we've harvested based on our own mental outcomes is enough to warrant action. At some point, our take-away from the road sign experience is binary: YES— I will do something with this information or NO—I will not do something with this information.

As we become versed at what Scripture explains will happen in the end times, we should make a note stack of all these pieces and perceptions so that we know the signs for which to watch. Why does God give us prophecy? It's to help us perceive so we can prepare. It's to help us see so we can trust Him. It's to help us see so that we can stay on track. God wants us to be prepared. This is the obvious theme through the remaining parables of Matthew 24 and 25.

Please take note of a few more very important thoughts before we continue our journey.

### Great Tribulation

First, "those days" are also identified by the phrase "the great tribulation" in verse 21. Let's read Mt 24:21-22 together again:

> *21For then shall be great tribulation, such as was not since the beginning of the world to this time, no, nor ever shall be. 22And except those days should be shortened, there should no flesh be saved: but for the elect's sake those days shall be shortened.*

For "then shall be great tribulation...." When is *then*? Isn't it interesting how we keep coming back to "then" and having to figure out what "then" means?! For "then shall be great tribulation..." is based on the same criteria as "those days" – a period beginning with the appearing of the abomination of desolation and moving forward. "Then" equals "those days" in Mt 24:21-22. Further, "then" is also defined as a period in which "great tribulation" will happen. So, if you were looking at this illustratively, you would see this: "then" = "those days" and inside "those days" will occur "great tribulation." That means that great tribulation will be inside "those days" for some length of time. The time of "great tribulation" doesn't appear to be the exact same length as "those days" but somewhat less because the great tribulation appears to start after "those days" have already begun, to end before "those days" are over, or perhaps it will be shorter on both ends. Two reasons this seems believable are: 1) Mt 24:21 says "then shall be great tribulation" where "then" is referencing the time frame from the abomination of desolation forward and "shall be" is an expectation to see the event: this suggests that in those days the event is expected, not synonymous; 2) Jesus says "then shall be great tribulation, such as was not…nor ever shall be" where "nor ever shall be" suggests that the great tribulation period has an end to it that does not end with time; whether the great tribulation period ends before Jesus returns to rule the earth is unknown, we just know that it will stop at some point.

*What Scripture Says Without Saying It*

Here is another place where Scripture speaks without using direct language. Consider Mt 24:22:

> [22]*And except those days should be shortened, there should no flesh be saved: but for the elect's sake those days shall be shortened.*

Let's start with the word *shortened* before we move ahead. The word in Greek[27] means "to amputate; to curtail;

---

[27] κολοβόω pronounced as kol-ob-o'-o (Strongs G2856)

to maim" in Dutch it's interestingly translated "to bring to an abrupt end." In all cases, the word reflects an expected length of something that is then reduced in size by cutting off the end of the expected length.

Considering the definition of *shortened,* the phrase "except those days should be shortened" becomes even more interesting because it seems to convey two possible thoughts: 1) that God has mercy on the world because the elect are still present in the world, and so God intervenes and stops the length of possible destruction before it's finally and fully complete; or 2) that God removes the elect out of destruction before the full days of destruction planned for the rest of the world are fully complete. In the second consideration, this could be a reference to the catching away of the elect from the earth, where Jesus gathers the elect to be with him at the first resurrection.

In either case, irrespective of which is true, one strong point exists: the elect are on the earth through some of the prescribed days identified as "those days" since the idea of "shortened" means all parties go the same direction with an intended shared and equal length, but where at some point, the journey of days is shortened and becomes less than originally expected.

In the first case, the elect are with the un-elect through all days as a shared experience and God shortens them for all because of the elect, which seems illogical and doesn't appear to agree with the rest of Scripture. In the second case, the elect leave before the end of the days allocated to the un-elect. One time frame we do know, however, is that the un-elect experience the beast-man's extreme rule for 1,290 days according to Daniel 12, and Rev 12:14 states he rules for "time, times and half a time" which is 3½ years. Time, times and a half time can also be 1,290 days if the Jewish year falls just right: more on this later.

It is upon consideration of the difference in experienced days that some may argue regarding the catching away of the elect by saying, "But the Scripture doesn't say how much shorter the days will be for the elect" and I think we should make note of this: Scripture does not say how much shorter—here—but, as we continue studying more detail exists. Also, the idea of truncating the days means there must be enough days shared to establish some level of common length, with an expectation of sharing all of them, or we can't say they were "truncated."

Based on what I see in Scripture, I believe scenario two is what Scripture represents: that the elect leave earlier than the un-elect, but the un-elect remain. Either way, we cannot escape that the elect begin a journey with those who are not elect, that both people groups are on the same road headed the same direction for a period and that during that time, both share the same events. We also cannot get away from the fact that these days *begin* with the appearing of the abomination of desolation. Consider these words from Paul in this regard. The following verses are retrieved from 2Thes 2:1-4:

> *¹Now we beseech you, brethren, by the coming of our Lord Jesus Christ, and [by] our gathering together unto him, ²That ye be not soon shaken in mind, or be troubled, neither by spirit, nor by word, nor by letter*

*as from us, as that the day of Christ is at hand. ³Let no man deceive you by any means: for [that day shall not come], except there come a falling away first, and that man of sin be revealed, the son of perdition; ⁴who opposeth and exalteth himself above all that is called God, or that is worshipped; so that he as God sitteth in the temple of God, showing himself that he is God.*

The only way Jesus appearing can happen is that first, the man of sin be revealed. The phrase "the man of sin" is a direct reference to the beast-man. Paul understood that the day of Jesus' return would not happen until after two things: 1) there will be a great apostasy from faith in God and 2) the beast-man will be revealed in the holy place, here called the "temple."

Remember that the word *temple* does not have to mean a big building: it is not necessary for the third full and complete temple to be rebuilt in Jerusalem for this to occur. We discussed this on previous pages and will discuss it even more in future ones. Remember this event must happen in a space where worship of God is performed. The word *temple*[28] here means just the innermost part of the temple, the holy place, and not the entire building itself. In heathen temples, it was only the enclosure that housed the physical idol. This word references only the holy place where the priests officiate their duties.

So, as of right now, we only see Scripture showing that the elect are here at the time the man of sin is revealed and consequently, according to Mt 24, when the abomination of desolation is also revealed. As a matter of fact, it is most

---

[28] ναός pronounced nah-os' (Strongs G3485)

likely that the placement of the abomination of desolation is how we finally know who the beast-man is! Nothing yet suggests the elect will be gone before this point. Will we see any moving forward? There's only one way to know.

### Who Are the Elect in These Verses?

If you've studied this in the past, you may be retorting with any of the following comments: "But those are the tribulation saints: We aren't here during that" or "Those are people who became Jesus' followers during the tribulation period" or "This can't be the pre-tribulation church because the word 'church' is never used in the Revelation during this time or after chapter 3." Before we move ahead, let's discuss this last idea. Allow me to offer an example for your consideration. Read the following and let me know what you think:

> *Dear Cousins. It has been 12 years since we've had a reunion and it's time we get back together. What do you think about the following activities? The zoo on Monday morning; coffee at Echo after that; supper at Marco's Italian in the evening; Tuesday morning coffee at Slingers and then the rest of the day at the lake. People can leave when the sun sets.*

Answer a few questions after reading that paragraph: 1) To whom was the paragraph written? What was your answer? If you said "cousins" then you were correct. The paragraph begins with "Dear Cousins" so from that, we know the author's cousins were the intended recipients. Next, what activities are described? Your answer? If you said: zoo, coffee at Echo, Marco's Italian, coffee at Slingers and the lake, you are again correct. Those were the activities listed above. Third, when is it over? Your answer? If you said "when the sun sets on Tuesday" you would be correct. Finally, who is/are identified as the participants in the activities? Your answer? If you said, "cousins" how do you know you're correct? I never once said the word cousins after the introduction of "Dear Cousins." Further, I only asked what they thought about the events, I never exclaimed they were invited. And lastly, I never said the cousins were done at sunset, I specifically used the word "people" as the subject of the last sentence.

Is it necessary for me to use the word cousins all through the paragraph for you to use your intellect and context to understand? If I had asked, "Who are the participants?" and someone answered "The residents of Montana" because they really want Montanans to be involved in the events, would you have thought it weird? But what if the term "cousin" is a common term for *friends* in Montana as it is in other geographic areas, would that have convinced you otherwise? Likely not. You would have to *want to believe* the term "cousin" was a general term for Montanans and you would have to *want to believe* the paragraph applied to those Montanans. The structure of the paragraph above is exactly what we see in the book of the Revelation. The book begins with letters to the churches and a declaration that God gave the Revelation to Jesus Himself so that He could give it to the church. In the end of the Revelation, we read Rev 22:16 which exclaims:

> *[16]I Jesus have sent mine angel to testify unto you these things in the churches....*

We see in the conclusion of the book that the intent of the book is to communicate to the churches just as it was declared at the beginning of the book. The Revelation of Jesus begins and ends as communication to the churches.

Why do we struggle to believe everything in between applies to the churches? Perhaps you are not convinced, and that is fine, but my challenge to you is to ask three things of yourself: 1) On what are you basing your belief, and have you tried to disprove it? 2) Why did Jesus warn us in Luke 21:8 to be wary of people saying Jesus' return will be sooner than it is in reality? 3) What if you're wrong in your possible assumption that the church is not here during lengths of the end days tribulation period? If you are wrong, and you bypass all that I have offered here, you could be sorely unprepared and so could your family and friends. At a minimum it is to your benefit to assume you can be wrong, to prepare, to become what God wants you to become. Then, if you never need to rely on your preparation—you've lost nothing. However, if you are wrong and you believe others who tell you not to be concerned, you have lost everything. In a moment, we will see that the idea of preparation is exactly what Jesus *drives* home in the coming parables.

The Beast – the Son of Perdition – Who is He?

Before we depart this section, there is one more major point that Scripture discusses without specifically speaking of it revolving around the beast-man. This is something we can't pass by. You saw previously in 2Thes 2:1-4 that the beast-man, the man behind the abomination of desolation discussed by Jesus in Mt 24 and in Daniel's writings, is called the "man of sin" by Paul in 1Thes 2:3. What else does Paul call this man? Paul calls him "the son of perdition" in the same verse. I believe this is the Holy Spirit giving us a foreshadow of what to expect with this man. You see, in a bit, we will learn more of how the man of sin is involved with the abomination of desolation being placed in the holy place of Jerusalem, but right here, we have a very strong hint about what he my look like before his revealing.

The phrase "son of perdition" only appears twice in the entirety of Scripture. The first time is in John 17:12 and the other time is here. Paul seemed to understand that the person spoken of by Jesus in John 17:12 was the same person or type of person spoken of in 1 Thes 2:3 because no one else in Scripture is given this title except for these two people. Who is the other person given this title if it's not the beast-man who exalts himself to be God, sitting in the temple of God declaring himself to be God? Who is the other man earning the title "son of perdition"? Let's read the words of Jesus Himself to understand. We go to John 17:1-12 as Jesus experiences His final hours before reaching His crucifixion:

> *[1]These words spake Jesus, and lifted up his eyes to heaven, and said, Father, the hour is come; glorify thy Son, that thy Son also may glorify thee: [2]As thou hast given him power over all flesh, that he should give eternal life to as many as thou hast given him. [3]And this is life eternal, that they might know thee the only true God, and Jesus Christ, whom thou hast sent. [4]I have glorified thee on the earth: I have finished the work which thou gavest me to do. [5]And now, O Father, glorify thou me with thine own self with the glory which I had with thee before the world was.*

> *[6]I have manifested thy name unto the men which thou gavest me out of the world: thine they were, and thou gavest them me; and they have kept thy word. [7]Now they have known that all things whatsoever thou hast given me are of thee. [8]For I have given unto them the words which thou gavest me; and they have received [them], and have known surely that I came*

*out from thee, and they have believed that thou didst*
*send me.*

*⁹I pray for them: I pray not for the world, but for*
*them which thou hast given me; for they are thine.*
*¹⁰And all mine are thine, and thine are mine; and I*
*am glorified in them. ¹¹And now I am no more in the*
*world, but these are in the world, and I come to thee.*
*Holy Father, keep through thine own name those*
*whom thou hast given me, that they may be one, as*
*we [are]. ¹²While I was with them in the world, I kept*
*them in thy name: those that thou gavest me I have*
*kept, and none of them is lost, but the son of*
*perdition; that the Scripture might be fulfilled.*

Here, we observe two different entities Jesus is
discussing: we have a group and an individual. About whom
is Jesus speaking in this section of Scripture? The group
He's referencing is the group of the twelve apostles. Jesus
makes this plain as we read His words in verses six through
nine as He identifies this group with phrases like: "the men
which thou gavest me out of the world," "I have given unto
them the words which thou gavest me; and they have
received," and "all mine are thine, and thine are mine; and I
am glorified in them." This whole piece of John 17 records
Jesus' words about the apostles, but who is the one, singular
individual whom Jesus discusses? Of the 12, who was the
one that was lost? Judas Iscariot. Judas was the one that
was lost out of all the disciples. Let's read what happened a
few chapters earlier in John 13:21-27:

*²¹When Jesus had thus said, he was troubled in*
*spirit, and testified, and said, Verily, verily, I say*
*unto you, that one of you shall betray me. ²²Then the*

*disciples looked one on another, doubting of whom he spake.*

*23Now there was leaning on Jesus' bosom one of his disciples, whom Jesus loved. 24Simon Peter therefore beckoned to him, that he should ask who it should be of whom he spake.*

*25He then lying on Jesus' breast saith unto him, Lord, who is it?*

*26Jesus answered, He it is, to whom I shall give a sop, when I have dipped [it]. And when he had dipped the sop, he gave [it] to Judas Iscariot, [the son] of Simon. 27And after the sop satan entered into him. Then said Jesus unto him, That thou doest, do quickly.*

Here we see that satan entered Judas and Judas then betrayed Jesus to death. The question we should likely ask is, "Why, out of all the titles and descriptions that exist, would the Holy Spirit prompt Paul to title the man of sin, the beast-man, as *the son of perdition* when the only other person in all of Scripture to have the same title is Judas Iscariot?" I think the answer is because he wants us to parallel the two. If this is the case, that the Holy Spirit wants us to understand the man of sin, the son of perdition, the beast-man, will be like Judas, then we should expect the beast-man to have the following characteristics: he will appear to be a Jesus-follower—by outward appearance he will be a disciple; he will be in a religiously and culturally influencing role; he will be esteemed among other people in the Christian circles; he will be a quiet thief; the appearance he has of helping the poor will actually only be to his benefit;

he will twist people's perceptions to believe he is genuine when he is actually a conspirator; he will be in a position of importance and leadership; he will be numbered among others who are sincere Jesus-followers; at the last minute, he will spin on a dime, be possessed by satan and will betray Jesus (in the end-times this will be the elect of God) and he will do all he can to make certain Jesus in and through the elect of God are murdered.

I believe the reason the man of sin, the son of perdition, the beast-man is titled with the same title as Judas Iscariot is because the Holy Spirit is warning us that if we are not paying attention, we will accept a seemingly well-meaning, "Jesus follower" if we are not discerning and watching for this pattern. I believe we are told, without being specifically told, that the beast-man will start out looking like a Jesus follower, but who is actually a liar, a thief and a destroyer who will turn on the elect of God, hate them and destroy them.

---

**Prophecy Watch**: The beast-man to come is called "the son of perdition" just as Judas Iscariot was, and we should be aware that he will possibly look like a Jesus follower when he appears, but that he is a liar, thief and murderer. We must exercise discernment before we put our faith in leaders.

---

## Pulling It Together (Mt 24:15-22)

What are the takeaway points? The "then" in Mt 24:21 appears to be the same time frame as "those days" in Mt 24:22. This period begins with the appearance of the abomination of desolation and ends much later. Sometime after the appearing of the abomination of desolation, from Jesus' sense of urgency, we would say very quickly after, the days of "great tribulation" begin. At this point, given what we can observe from Jesus' words, we can assume it will be a timeframe lasting greater than two months given the difficulties pregnant and nursing mothers will experience. How much longer, we don't yet know: that part of the journey is reserved to learn, if possible, as we continue excavating truth from the Scriptures. For certain, however, we know from Jesus' words in the gospels that the time of great tribulation will have an end, but the gospels don't say when that will be; and finally, the elect will experience an indeterminate portion of days with the rest of the word since they will experience a "shortened" or truncated version of those days, but without definition on how much shorter in Mt 24.

We also learned that before this time, there will be a falling away of people from their faith and that the world leader who is behind the placing of the abomination of desolation in the holy place will possibly follow the pattern of Judas Iscariot: seeming to be a Jesus follower, he will turn 180 degrees in one moment and become the largest enemy of the elect of God, seeking their death. We learned that the holy place, also called the temple, does not mean the entire building is required, but that it could as easily be a marked-off area set aside for the worship of God. Finally, we learned that the tamid, the daily worship practice and likely the daily sacrifice, must be a current practice because it is stopped by the beast-man at the placing of the abomination of desolation.

---

**Prophecy Watch**: The appearance of the abomination of desolation is a pinnacle fact in Scripture that Jesus presents as visible, obvious, defining and warning.

---

# When is Jesus Coming?

As we've seen, the first 22 verses of Matthew 24 are filled with interesting information about the time leading up to the great tribulation, the persecution of God's elect, the killing of the same, betrayal between family and friends, the spirit of iniquity and lawlessness that becomes more pervasive, people defending their selves on fear of death from others and the ultimate spread of the gospel of Jesus to the entire world. If these points don't sound familiar, go back and review the *Pulling it Together* sections to refresh your memory. We are gaining momentum and our remembering what we've discovered to this point is paramount to our understanding of what is next.

## Here a Christ, There a Christ (Mt 24:23-28)

As we step into Matthew 24:23 we must remember we are following on the heels of Mt 24:21-22. Let's re-read verses 23-25 and add these two verses in front of them so we have context.

*²¹For then shall be great tribulation²⁹, such as was not since the beginning of the world to this time, no, nor ever shall be. ²²And except those days should be shortened, there should no flesh be saved: but for the elect's sake those days shall be shortened. ²³Then if any man shall say unto you, Lo, here [is] Christ, or there; believe [it] not. ²⁴For there shall arise false Christs, and false prophets, and shall shew great signs and wonders; insomuch that, if [it were] possible, they shall deceive the very elect. ²⁵Behold, I have told you before.*

For "then" shall be great tribulation, at, or very shortly after, the revealing of the abomination of desolation. This tribulation will be unlike any in history and will last for a determined period, although the gospels don't tell us the length. Either the elect will experience fewer of these days, or the entire world will experience fewer of them because of the elect, but they will be cut short for or because of the elect. This is where we pick up verse 23.

Here we have another "then." There are lots of *thens* aren't there?! Again, we must discern: does "then" mean during the time period we are discussing or after the time period we are discussing (go back to the section titled *Start with Jesus* and read about "then" if you don't remember this conversation). Here, the antecedent (the focus before the "then") is Jesus words "…but for the elect's sake, those days shall be shortened." We just learned the term "those days"

---

²⁹ The word *tribulation* here is the same Greek word as *afflicted* in Mt 24:9, it is the word θλῖψις pronounced thlip'-sis (Strongs G2347) and it means tribulation, affliction, trouble, anguish and persecution.

references the days of great tribulation. So "then" here is also and still referencing the days of great tribulation.

Jesus warns us that during the great tribulation period "if any man shall say unto you, Lo, here is Christ, or there; believe it not." Jesus warns people in those days from two millennia ago. **During the greatest trial, those suffering will look for the greatest hope.** Jesus knows those on earth will need hope, will look for hope, and will want a way to bring the tribulation to an end. He also knows that He is the only one who can bring hope. Further, *Jesus knows that the elect know* He is the only one who can bring all these events to an end. More than ever, the elect will want Jesus to return to bring the age to an end. Jesus knows this and says, "…if any man shall say unto you, Lo, here is Christ, or there; believe it not."

Just to confirm this understanding, let's put on our critical thinking hat. God is logical. Jesus proves God is logical by His myriad discourses. If the world *hates* Jesus (Jn 17) and the world hates the elect (Jn 17), and if the elect are hated by all nations for Jesus' name sake (Mt 24:9), it stands to reason that the world is not in love with Jesus, does not want Him or His influence and wants to eradicate Him and His influence: both Him and the elect. This is very plain from Scripture. Given the hatred toward Jesus and those that belong to Jesus, who else but the elect would care favorably if Jesus was returning? And who else but the elect would be watching for Him in anticipation? Jesus, in Mt 24:23 is talking to listeners who are looking for His return because He's warning this future group of people not to believe it is Him! He doesn't want them to be confused or to get their hopes up unnecessarily. Certainly, the world wouldn't care one bit.  "But wait" you may be thinking.  "That Scripture doesn't specifically say it's the elect.  What if it's the non-elect watching for Him so they can destroy him?!"  Let's look at the next verse of Matthew 24:

> *24For there shall arise false Christs, and false prophets, and shall shew great signs and wonders; insomuch that, if [it were] possible, they shall deceive the very elect.*

In this verse, Jesus begins layering additional detail to His teaching.  "For there shall arise false Christs, and false prophets…[attempting to] deceive the very elect."  Jesus is very plain here.  The assault is against the "very elect."  It is the "very elect" who are looking for His coming; the "very elect" who are the target of deception.  The non-elect aren't the target of deception because they don't care; they don't need to be deceived because they are already deceived.  It is the very elect who *want* Jesus to come back and to end all that is happening, and **it is the very elect who are susceptible to deception at this point because their desire can outweigh their discernment.**  Jesus says, "…believe it not" (Mt 24:23).  Then Jesus ends this specific thought in Matthew 24 with these keystone words:

> *25Behold, I have told you before.*

Jesus is speaking from ~AD30 and telling the elect who will live over two millennia in the future that they must pay attention.  Jesus knew what would happen, he knows the heart of man and how badly the elect will crave His return, and He's making it clear.

As we jump into Mt 24:26-28 we have quite a picture painted for us as Jesus explains the extremism that will befall the elect as they look for His return. Again, remember, this is a warning to people longing for Jesus' coming. Let's read together:

> *26Wherefore if they shall say unto you, Behold, he is in the desert; go not forth: behold, [he is] in the secret chambers; believe [it] not. 27For as the lightning cometh out of the east, and shineth even unto the west; so shall also the coming of the Son of man be. 28For wheresoever the carcass is, there will the eagles be gathered together.*

During this time, when things are very difficult and the elect want Jesus to return and bring all end-times events to a conclusion, Jesus warns the elect that they will hear about false sightings of His return happening in the desert and in secret chambers. What this suggests is that people will travel wherever they must to find Jesus because they want to see Him that badly and believe they perceive Him to be the answer to everything happening. All this running around, Jesus says, is unnecessary since His coming will be obvious to the entire world.

Then we end up with Mt 24:28 which is a point of quandary for us. We'll see that this appears to tie into Revelation 19 when we arrive there, but Jesus says this: when I return, it will be obvious, and "wheresoever the carcass is, there will the eagles be gathered together." That seems like a very cryptic statement, only made more difficult because Eagles are fresh meat creatures: eagles don't typically eat animals that have already been killed. Vultures are creatures who clean up dead things. You've seen this, likely while driving on the freeway. A critter is hit by a car and the vultures come and pick the flesh off the bones. How often have you seen an eagle sitting on the highway, eating a dead deer or opossum? Vultures like dead meat: eagles, seldom if ever eat carrion. Let's dig into what this could mean, again, using deductive reasoning and our pursuit of Scripture as a guide.

## Wheresoever the Carcass Is (Mt 24:28)

This phrase, "…wheresoever the carcass is, there will the eagles be gathered together" created quite a bit of thought and digging as I was processing how it fit in the end times. Let's break it down piece by piece and evaluate it.

### What is the context?

The context of this verse is defined in Mt 24:21-27, specifically associated to these events: the presentation of the abomination of desolation, the ensuing days of great tribulation, the attempted deceiving of the elect by false Christs and false prophets, people saying Jesus has returned when in reality He hasn't; and a reminder that when Jesus does appear, it will be obvious. Because the last thing said before

*[28] …wheresoever the carcass is…*

happens to be

*<sup>27</sup>For as the lightning cometh out of the east, and shineth even unto the west; so shall also the coming of the Son of man be.*

The immediate perception for many seems to be the following sequence of thought:

*Jesus is coming in the clouds! The elect are gathered together to meet Him in the air when He does! Eagles are stately, honorable and glorious creatures who dominate the skies! We are the eagles, gathering to Jesus at his return.*

Perhaps you've thought the same. Let's look at what we must accept for this to be true. First, if the elect are represented by the eagles gathering together, that would make Jesus the *carcass* because

*<sup>28</sup>...wheresoever the carcass is, there will the eagles be gathered together.*

Calling Jesus, or Jesus calling Himself, a carcass seems a bit insulting. While it is true that He did die, He also is the firstborn from the dead through resurrection (Col 1:18) and He is far from dead meat. Jesus is not a carcass; he is a living man. But what if we adopt the idea that it is merely metaphorical? If we intend to say that Scripture means something it doesn't specifically say, we should find other examples in Scripture to verify our potential understanding. There are many times where metaphor is used in Scripture, but to make a sound doctrine about that metaphor, we can't merely rely on one verse and our own personal wish for it to be true: that is a very dangerous practice. Where else do we see Jesus referenced or referencing Himself as a carcass?

How often is the term carcass used to identify a metaphor that is good? Let's look and see.

## The Carcass

Looking in the Old Testament for a carcass and how it's used, whether metaphorically or with concrete intent, shows the following:

- A carcass makes anyone who touches it unclean[30]: Lev 5:2, 11:8, 11:24-28, 35-40; Jer 31:40
- We are not to eat part of a carcass or any animal that feeds on a carcass: Deut 14:8; Jdg 14:8-9
- Public exposure of a carcass is a curse against the deceased person and/or a person being reduced to a carcass is a judgment against the individual because they are or were wicked or sinned against God: Lev 26:30; Num 14:29-33; Deut 28:26; Jos 8:29; 1Sam 17:46; 1Sam 31:10-12; 1Ki 13:22-30; 2Ki 19:35-37; 2Chr 20:24-25; Ps 110:6; Is 14:19; Is 34:3, 37:36; Is 66:24; Jer 33:5; Jer 41:9; Eze 6:5; Eze 43:7-9; Amos 8:3; Nah 3:3

The list above represents all Old Testament scriptures that identify and deal with the term *carcass*. There are two Hebrew words that are translated as carcass[31] and in all cases of both Hebrew words, the meaning is negative or would represent a state of impurity that would never represent

---

[30] The term *unclean* references a Jewish worshiper's ability to enter into God's presence; an unclean person cannot worship until he or she is made clean again. Uncleanness to the Jew is undesired and fully disrupts their formal worship of God.

[31] גְּוִיָּה which is pronounced ghev-ee-yaw' (Strongs H1472) and פֶּגֶר which is pronounced peh'gher (Strongs H6297).

Jesus as the pure and spotless Passover sacrifice[32]. And lest we fall prey to the old argument of "well that was the Old Testament" let's please remember a few key takeaway points dealing with that line of reasoning. First:

> [16]*All Scripture [is] given by inspiration of God, and [is] profitable for doctrine, for reproof, for correction, for instruction in righteousness: [17]That the man of God may be perfect, thoroughly furnished unto all good works. – 2Tim 3:16-17*

The purpose of Scripture, all that we have in the Old Testament, is to instruct us on the heart, mind, thoughts and attitudes of God as well as to instill wisdom, instruct in righteousness and as examples of how to process all applicable understandings.

We must also remember:

> [6]*For I [am] the LORD, I change not; therefore ye sons of Jacob are not consumed. – Mal 3:6*

The Lord God does not change, neither does Jesus:

> [8]*Jesus Christ the same yesterday, and to day, and for ever. – Heb 13:8*

We cannot allow ourselves to discount things we don't like about Scripture on the argument that grace has changed everything. God's heart hasn't changed about any of the things He doesn't like. If He didn't like something in the Old Testament, He still doesn't like it in the New Testament. He may not execute judgment the same way or at the same

---

[32] See my book *The Crucifixion: Was it Friday? Does it matter?* for detailed interaction on this topic.

time, but His heart hasn't changed. And for anyone who loves Him, we would do well to remember: God's heart still hurts when we do things that He hates.

So where does this leave us regarding the word *carcass?* In the Old Testament, the term *carcass* is not used positively, it represents judgement when applied to people, and touching a carcass makes a person unclean, requiring them to perform a sacrifice, a washing or some action accompanied with a waiting period to possibly become clean again.

Now that we know the Old Testament representation of *carcass*, let's look at the New Testament use of the word. The Greek has one word[33] used to represent the term and it is used in the following ways:

- A mere reference to a dead man: Mk 6:29
- Reference to dead bodies lying in the streets being refused burial for 3½ days: Rev 11:8-9; akin to the Old Testament use to shame individuals.

That's it. The only other use in the Bible that we have not covered is our target verse in Mt 24:28, and that is the one we are trying to understand.

Allowing Scripture to interpret Scripture, we see that in the entirety of Scripture, the term *carcass* is used to represent: a dead body in general, which Jesus is not; a gateway to uncleanness requiring cleansing if touched by mankind, again, not Jesus; something that could be eaten but that we should not eat because it will cause us to become unclean, yet again, not Jesus; a representation of cursing and judgment because of a person's sin or wickedness, still not

---

[33] πτῶμα pronounced pto'-mah (Strongs G4430)

Jesus; a judgment of mankind against an individual to shame him or her—even this can't be Jesus because mankind has nothing to do with His appearing the second time, or an ability to shame Him or destroy Him at his coming.

Allowing Scripture to interpret Scripture, we could only claim that Jesus is the *carcass* in Mt 24:28 because we choose to interpret it that way for our own personal doctrine or gain. Scripture not only fails to support the idea that Jesus is the metaphorical carcass, it actually refutes the idea.

Now, if Jesus isn't the carcass, then who or what is and what is Jesus talking about in Mt 24:28? It is fully possible that this is completely metaphor and that this is the only occurrence in Scripture of the metaphor and that even though a carcass never fits Jesus in any other way, it still references Him; albeit, I find that doubtful. I do believe that Scripture answers this question in the Revelation, and I feel confident we'll see the answer as we move ahead. If you feel adventuresome, we'll discuss this more in Mt 24:36-44 with some other possibilities in Rev 14 and Rev 19. For now, let's continue to allow Scripture to interpret Scripture, and since we have no basis in Scripture to believe Jesus is the carcass, let's lay this aside and come back to it in a bit.

## After the Carcass (Mt 24:29)

After the carcass, we jump into some very definitive Scripture on Jesus' appearing. It is super important to move ahead reminding ourselves that if Jesus isn't the carcass in verse 28, that someone or something else must be and that since the carcass is a sign of judgment and shame, not to mention physical death, there is a person or there are people who will fulfill this scripture: a person or people will die, and birds will feed on their flesh. As harsh as that may sound, this begins a fuller understanding of how much death and destruction we will see as we enter the end times. You may not fully grasp how deadly a time is ahead for planet Earth. When Jesus says this will be a time of tribulation unlike the world has ever seen before, or will see, He is being serious. If you can imagine all the bloodshed of the worst circumstances, possibly World War II as a point of reference, the great tribulation period will surpass that death toll by more than 75 times. When our journey takes us into the Revelation, I have a chart of death statistics I will share that are derived from Scripture. Let me say now, however, the death toll in the end-times is extensive.

So, what is next? Jesus begins to address that question in Mt 24:29-44. Let's look at the verse 29 by itself first:

> *29Immediately after the tribulation of those days shall the sun be darkened, and the moon shall not give her light, and the stars shall fall from heaven, and the powers of the heavens shall be shaken:*

Here we have the phrase "those days" so we need to start by discerning what "those days" refers to. If you recall, we first experienced "those days" in Mt 24:19. There, we determined that "those days" refers to the time just after the appearing of the abomination of desolation and going forward to a point that Mt 24 did not disclose, but that must be months at a minimum. We also must understand that other Scriptures fill in this blank for us, Daniel 12 being one of them; but, for now, let's settle with what we have in Mt 24: it begins at the appearing of the abomination of desolation and goes forward months. Here in Mt 24:29, we must now discern if "those days" are the same period as before or a different period altogether. Jesus makes this easy for us, because He specifically states "Immediately after the tribulation of those days" which seems to be pointing to the same days referenced in verse 21:

*²¹For then shall be great tribulation, such as was not since the beginning of the world to this time, no, nor ever shall be.*

Those days are days of great tribulation in verse 21 and immediately after those days, we see that verse 29 tells us what is next.

*²⁹Immediately after the tribulation of those days shall the sun be darkened, and the moon shall not give her light, and the stars shall fall from heaven, and the powers of the heavens shall be shaken:*

Immediately; on the heels of. One way the Greek reads is "Forthwith then with" or just as soon as those days come to a closing point, the sun will be darkened, the moon will not shine, the stars of the heaven will fall, and the powers of the heavens will be shaken. This is a very simple representation of what will occur: Jesus is just making the point that it will be universal and identifiable.

Interestingly, another way Mt 24:29 can be translated is "Immediately with[34] the tribulation of the same[35] days"[36]

---

[34] μετά pronounced as met-ah' (Strongs G3326) which is also translated: with, after, among, behind and against.

[35] ἐκεῖνος pronounced as ek-i'-nos (Strongs G1565) which is also translated: that, those, he, the same, they and other ways.

[36] The question must be asked: did the translators determine Jesus' perspective was historical or contemporary to determine their translation. They took a historical view of His words, as if He was seeing all things as complete. What if Jesus is stating His words from inside the days? The perspective of Jesus could shift the words

signifying that the signs we just discussed *could be* contemporaneous with the beginning of the great tribulation period. This could mean that the sun being darkened, the moon being darkened and the stars falling from heaven, as well as the gathering of the elect to Jesus, happens sometime with or relatively after the abomination of desolation is revealed. We will need to rely on the rest of Scripture to answer this question. Irrespective, we know one thing to be true in both possible scenarios: the elect are not gathered to Jesus until after the abomination of desolation is revealed. Regarding whether that time is earlier or later, let's see where we land as we continue our study.

Beyond much concern or doubt, this series of events ties Mt 24 together with the book of the Revelation and is one of the ways we know that Jesus is speaking about the same events in the Revelation. We will see these same events discussed again at the sixth seal of Rev 6:12-17. The fact that I'm speaking of the sixth seal may not ring a bell yet but keep going: it will make sense before you're done, and we'll interact with this a bit more in coming pages.

## Pulling It Together (Mt 24:23-29)

Jesus' coming to gather His elect will be obvious and the entire world will see it and know when it happens. The elect won't have to guess and won't have to be concerned that they've somehow missed the catching away or that they must chase after Jesus. When the time is right, Jesus Himself will come to gather His elect and at the same time there appears to be a great death event. Jesus states at His

---

"immediately after...those days" to "immediately with...these days" and it appears both would be correct since both are possessive in the Greek.

94

coming that there will also be a set of circumstances that includes the term carcass and birds eating carrion. Matthew 24:28 states:

> [28]*for wheresoever the carcass is, there will the eagles be gathered together.*

We have no scriptural reason to believe that the *carcass* is Jesus and that the elect are the eagles being gathered to Him. In all of Scripture, every instance of the word *carcass* would not open the door to this understanding, instead, every use of *carcass* is in a negative sense and since eagles don't eat carrion, we must assume the translation of this word should be along the lines of vulture for it to fit with the subject of carcass. This appears to be a warning of a judgment that will happen, which we will delve into more in the coming pages.

# The Sign, Gathering and Fig

This may seem like a strange place to begin a new chapter, but there is good reason. We have two events that we cannot confuse: one is found in Matthew 24 and the other in Matthew 25. In Matthew 24, we have *the sign of the Son of man* and in Matthew 25 we have *when the Son of man shall come in his glory.* These most definitely appear to be two different events and the whole of Scripture seems to support this. Let's review together.

## The Sign of the Son of Man (Mt 24:30-31)

Remember the amazing and cataclysmic events of Mt 24:29 that take place? The sun, moon and stars become dark, the stars fall from the sky and the heavens are shaken; then Scripture records what is next, starting with Matthew 24:30:

> *30 And then shall appear the sign of the Son of man in heaven: and then shall all the tribes of the earth mourn, and they shall see the Son of man coming in the clouds of heaven with power and great glory. 31 And he shall send his angels with a great sound of a trumpet, and they shall gather together his elect*

*from the four winds, from one end of heaven to the other.*

Here we see that the sun, moon and stars events ushers in the sign of the Son of man. What are the specific take-away points when this happens?

- The tribes of the earth mourn
- Jesus can be seen coming in the clouds of heaven
- Jesus is seen in power and great glory
- Jesus sends his angels with the great sound of a trumpet
- The angels gather the "…elect from the four winds, from one end of heaven to the other."

Notice that this section of Scripture does not reveal anything about the elect arriving with Jesus on the clouds of heaven; in actuality, we are told that the elect are being gathered to Him. This is very important.

---

**Prophecy Watch**: Matthew 24 does not state that the elect are with Jesus at the sign of His coming.

---

What else can we observe? The tribes of the earth mourn because of what they see: Jesus in the clouds with power and great glory. There is no discussion of judgment at this point, no discussion of death. What we see is a sign that is visible globally and includes Jesus gathering the elect from the four winds: from one end of heaven to the other.

Scripture seems very plain that this is different from Jesus' physical return: the sign of His coming is a spectacle, a sign visible to mankind proclaiming that Jesus is alive and not limited by this world; He is powerful, mighty and in control. This could be a vision that all mankind sees, or it could be a true optical experience. Let's consider another time in Scripture where Jesus was in His kingdom and was seen by just a *few* men.

Chapters earlier, we see these verses as recorded in Mt 16:28-17:3, 9:

> *Mt 16:28 Verily I say unto you, There be some standing here, which shall not taste of death, till they see the Son of man coming in his kingdom. 17:1 And after six days Jesus taketh Peter, James, and John his brother, and bringeth them up into an high mountain apart, 2And was transfigured before them: and his face did shine as the sun, and his raiment was white as the light. 3And, behold, there appeared unto them Moses and Elias talking with him. ... 9And as they came down from the mountain, Jesus charged them, saying, Tell the vision to no man, until the Son of man be risen again from the dead.*

In Mt 16:28, Jesus says that *some* standing there will see Him coming in His kingdom. The word "coming" can also be translated as "appearing" so perhaps this would be better understood as "...till they see the Son of man appearing in his kingdom." Certainly, people who were with Jesus will see His return at the resurrection; but since Matthew wrote these words on the heels of Jesus' interaction with Moses and Elijah, it seems most believable that Jesus and Matthew associated the two experiences together.

What is interesting about this account in Mt 16 and 17 is that for a brief period, Peter, James and John saw Jesus in another existence while simultaneously being physically in His earthly presence. This section of Scripture is identified as the *Mount of Transfiguration* because Jesus was transfigured before their eyes: He changed existence in front of them! He was no longer merely an earthly man, but He was now visible to these disciples in His heavenly kingdom: white, shining, like the sun! And while in His kingdom, He was interacting with Moses and Elijah, and the disciples were able to see and hear them interact with Jesus. And yet, Jesus identifies this experience to the disciples as a *vision* meaning the disciples had never physically changed locations or existences their selves. For a brief period, the disciples were allowed to see Jesus on earth as He already was in Heaven[37]: the spotless, glorious, Son of God. And lest we neglect to understand this fact, God punctuates the disciple's vision experience in verse five:

> *⁵While he* [Jesus] *yet spake, behold, a bright cloud overshadowed them: and behold a voice out of the cloud, which said, This is my beloved Son, in whom I am well pleased; hear ye him.*

We will compare and contrast *the sign of the Son* with *the coming of the Son* in much greater detail when we arrive in Mt 25, but for now, understand: the sign of the Son of man appears to be a supernatural event where the heavens roll back like a scroll, some verses lead us to believe that they are destroyed, and where mankind is able to see Jesus in His glory, on clouds and on His way to the earth. We don't know if the supernatural sign stays visible, or if the

---

[37] Jesus was simultaneously in Heaven and on Earth. While this is hard to understand in our four-dimensional minds (length, width, height and time), Jesus was and is not bound by the creation made through Him. Remember Jesus words: *And no man hath ascended up to heaven, but he that came down from heaven, [even] the Son of man which is in heaven – Jn 3:13.* Jesus explained to Nicodemus that, while He spoke to him on earth, He was already and simultaneously in heaven.

scroll closes, or what happens next, because Scripture never tells us; but this one thing we do know: we know that whatever the sign is, it's visible to the entire world because mankind across the face of the planet goes into mourning. We also know that it doesn't carry the same action points as His return to the earth and because of this, we know the sign of His coming is a totally separate occurrence from His coming. When we get to Mt 25, this will become even more obvious.

## Gathering the Elect

Now, back to Mt 24:30-31 and the sign of His appearing. As a reminder, let's re-read the two verses.

> *[30] And then shall appear the sign of the Son of man in heaven: and then shall all the tribes of the earth mourn, and they shall see the Son of man coming in the clouds of heaven with power and great glory. [31] And he shall send his angels with a great sound of a trumpet, and they shall gather together his elect from the four winds, from one end of heaven to the other.*

We cannot miss a very interesting fact in verse 31. Jesus states he is sending his angels to gather the elect from the four winds. What are the four winds? Scripture never specifically defines them, but in all occurrences of the phrase usage, it appears to be North, South, East and West[38]. Jesus also said the angels were gathering the elect from one

---

[38] See the following for all occurrences: Jer 49:36, Eze 37:9, Dan 7:2, Dan 8:8, Dan 11:4, Zec 2;6, MT 24:31, Mk 13:27, Rev 7:1

end of heaven to the other. This word for *heaven*[39] can mean both the heavens holding the stars, clouds and sky as well as the place where God currently dwells. Look at how Mark records these words of Jesus in his gospel found in Mark 13:27:

> *[27]And then shall he send his angels, and shall gather together his elect from the four winds, from the uttermost part of the earth to the uttermost part of heaven .*

I believe the reason we see both *the four winds,* which are part of our earthly creation, and *heaven* (Mark writes *"uttermost part of heaven"*), which is where God's throne resides, is because this gathering is of people already in Heaven and of people who are still on the earth: people are gathered from the four winds who have just been caught up into the clouds and they are reunited with those already in heaven; all to be with Jesus. I believe this represents fulfillment of Scripture as noted by Paul in 1Thes 4:16-17. See if you agree:

> *[16]For the Lord himself shall descend from heaven with a shout, with the voice of the archangel, and with the trump of God: and the dead in Christ shall rise first: [17]Then we which are alive [and] remain shall be caught up together with them in the clouds, to meet the Lord in the air: and so shall we ever be with the Lord.*

If we allow the Bible to interpret itself, we have a compelling case that these events are the same. Let's

---

[39] οὐρανός pronounced oo-ran-os' (Strongs G3772)

parallel the scriptures next to each other and compare details.

| Mt 24 | 1Thes 4 |
|---|---|
| 30And then shall appear the sign of the Son of man in heaven… | 16For the Lord himself shall descend from heaven… |
| 31And he shall send his angels with a great sound of a trumpet… | 16…with the voice of the archangel, and with the trump of God |
| 31…they shall gather together his elect from the four winds, from one end of heaven to the other.<br><br>Mk 13:27…from the uttermost part of the earth to the uttermost part of heaven. | 16…and the dead in Christ shall rise first: 17Then we which are alive [and] remain shall be caught up together with them in the clouds, to meet the Lord in the air |

As I noted earlier, this also seems to tie into the 6th seal of the Revelation (there are seven seals total). Let me introduce the verses to you from the book of the Revelation that relate to the 6th seal so you can read them yourself. We will just touch them now; we won't get into detail, but I want you to see them just the same. Here is Revelation 6:12-17:

*12And I beheld when he had opened the sixth seal, and, lo, there was a great earthquake; and the sun became black as sackcloth of hair, and the moon became as blood; 13And the stars of heaven fell unto the earth, even as a fig tree casteth her untimely figs, when she is shaken of a mighty wind. 14And the heaven departed as a scroll when it is rolled together; and every mountain and island were moved out of their places. 15And the kings of the earth, and the great men, and the rich men, and the chief captains, and the mighty men, and every*

102

*bondman, and every free man, hid themselves in the dens and in the rocks of the mountains; <sup>16</sup>And said to the mountains and rocks, Fall on us, and hide us from the face of him that sitteth on the throne, and from the wrath of the Lamb: <sup>17</sup>For the great day of his wrath is come; and who shall be able to stand?*

Compare this to Matthew 24:29-31. Let's do it in parallel again.

| Mt 24 | Rev 6 |
| --- | --- |
| <sup>29</sup>Immediately after the tribulation of those days shall the sun be darkened, and the moon shall not give her light… | <sup>12</sup>And I beheld when he had opened the sixth seal, and, lo, there was a great earthquake; and the sun became black as sackcloth of hair, and the moon became as blood |
| <sup>29</sup>…and the stars shall fall from heaven, and the powers of the heavens shall be shaken | <sup>13</sup>And the stars of heaven fell unto the earth, even as a fig tree casteth her untimely figs, when she is shaken of a mighty wind. <sup>14</sup>And the heaven departed as a scroll when it is rolled together; and every mountain and island were moved out of their places. |
| <sup>30</sup>And then shall appear the sign of the Son of man in heaven: and then shall all the tribes of the earth mourn, and they shall see the Son of many coming in the clouds of heaven with power and great glory. | <sup>15</sup>And the kings of the earth, and the great men, and the rich men, and the chief captains, and the mighty men, and every bondman, and every free man, hid themselves in the dens and in the rocks of the mountains; <sup>16</sup>And said to the mountains and rocks, Fall on us, and hide us from the face of him that sitteth on the throne, and from the wrath of the Lamb |

It is good to note that Revelation 6 does not discuss angels gathering the elect. It is also interesting that the phrase "...and every mountain and island were moved out of their places..." does not happen in Mt 24. Still, the evidence of both sections of Scripture seems to suggest that these are the one and same event, even with those two missing pieces.

The events of Mt 24 and the 6th seal in Rev 6 bring up a very interesting observation, specifically that Jesus' teachings in Mt 24:4-31 match the events of the seals of the Revelation; in absolute honesty, when I realized this, I was rather intrigued. Jesus tells us the seals of the Revelation in Matthew 24. This opens all sorts of thoughts and possibilities, many of which we will deal with when we get into the book of the Revelation itself.

## When? A Lesson From the Fig Tree (Mt 24:32-35)

In Matthew 24:32-35 Jesus inserts an understanding of the fig tree. Specifically, Jesus states it is a parable, a teaching in illustrative form. Here is what Jesus says:

> *32Now learn a parable of the fig tree; When his branch is yet tender, and putteth forth leaves, ye know that summer [is] nigh: 33So likewise ye, when ye shall see all these things, know that it is near, [even] at the doors. 34Verily I say unto you, This generation shall not pass, till all these things be fulfilled. 35Heaven and earth shall pass away, but my words shall not pass away.*

Jesus is associating the sign of His appearing, the sounding of the trumpet and the gathering of the elect with something the people understood very well from their own farms: fig trees. Now for you, perhaps it is an apple tree, or a pear tree, or perhaps a pecan tree or an orange tree or a mango tree, or even a grape vine. The idea is the same in any illustration: think of the fruit-bearing creation you know the best and follow along with the rest of the parable. All these trees and plants have a cycle: they begin to green, they sprout buds, leaves form, they blossom, they begin to bear fruit, the fruit begins to mature, and finally, the tree or plant is ready for harvest. You have a good idea about when each of these stages should happen. For grapes in the midsouth where I live, they start to sprout leaves in April-May, they continue to grow leaves and sprout vines, then in June and July we start to see the initial baby grapes. Then, August they are getting more visible and by September we are ready to start harvesting and depending on the season, even into October we are harvesting grapes.

Jesus' point is this: if you know the plant or the tree, you don't have to know the calendar to perceive the correct time of year. If you are familiar with the plant, it will tell you. When I see little baby grapes, I know it must be the middle to end of July. When they are ready to eat, I know it must be mid to late September. If every calendar on the world were destroyed, but I still had a grape vine in my backyard, I could tell the month by the plant. I could do the same thing with wheat or sorghum because these are plants I know well. Jesus is asking us this question: Do you know the signs of my appearing, the sounding of the trumpet and the gathering of the elect so well that you can tell the season you are in without being told or having to look on some "calendar"? Can you tell where you are in the end times by just watching the signs of the times?

## Pulling it Together (Mt 24:29-35)

Jesus' return appears to be in two parts. Matthew 24:1-28 explains the *sign of the Son of man* where we see the alert of His immanent return and Mt 24:29 through Mt 25:46 explains the   physical return and *coming of the Son of man*. We know these are two different events because their details are different and things that happen by *the coming of the Son* have not happened by *the sign of the Son*. We also know that the events of Mt 24:29-31 parallel the sixth seal of the Revelation and Paul's observations of what happens at Jesus appearing in 1Thessalonians 4.

We don't know if the sign of His coming is a vision that is seen by the entire world, such as what happened on the Mount of Transfiguration, or if it's a true ocular event, but we know that the world will indeed see Jesus coming on clouds in power and great glory and that the world will mourn. We know that at this time, Jesus will send his angels with the sound of a great trumpet to gather the elect from the four winds of the earth and the farthest reaches of Heaven itself.

Finally, we know from Jesus' teaching about the fig tree that He expects us to know these events so well that we can tell the season of His return without being dependent upon anyone or anything to tell us where we are in the end-times events. Just as we can watch the fig tree progress through its growing season as it matures and approaches fruit bearing, we can watch the signs of the times to know when Jesus is returning with nothing but the signs to guide us.

# Jesus is Coming

You have heard over and again that "no one knows the day or hour of Jesus' return" and this is true in practicality: we don't and won't. As a matter of fact, to make sure we are accurate as we move forward, lets read Jesus words together. Matthew 24:36 records:

> *36 But of that day and hour knoweth no [man], no, not the angels of heaven, but my Father only.*

Okay. There you have it. Only God knows the day and the hour of Jesus return. Really? Let's review to see if this is what Scripture really says. You probably knew I was going to do that, didn't you?

## No One Knows the Day or Hour (Mt 24:36)

To begin, we have another "that" again and we need to figure out "that" to which it points. As you recall, Jesus paused the prophetically historical event list to expound the parable of the fig tree. Let's remember the few verses before the fig tree parable.

*<sup>29</sup>Immediately after the tribulation of those days shall the sun be darkened, and the moon shall not give her light, and the stars shall fall from heaven, and the powers of the heavens shall be shaken: <sup>30</sup>And then shall appear the sign of the Son of man in heaven: and then shall all the tribes of the earth mourn, and they shall see the Son of man coming in the clouds of heaven with power and great glory. <sup>31</sup>And he shall send his angels with a great sound of a trumpet, and they shall gather together his elect from the four winds, from one end of heaven to the other.*

Just after this, Jesus steps into the parable of the fig tree, making certain we understand the importance of being able to tell the signs of His appearing, the sounding of the trumpet and the gathering of the elect, and then he continues with the following verse:

*<sup>36</sup>But of that day and hour no one knows, not even the angels of heaven, but My Father only.*

From this, we know the words "that day and hour" reference His appearing, the sounding of the trumpet and the gathering of the elect. This happens before His physical return. These verses are not dealing with Jesus physical return on the white horse as the king of all creation who will rule for 1,000 years with a rod of iron as Revelation 19 introduces. These verses are dealing with the day and hour that His sign appears, and the elect are gathered with the sound of the trumpet! We know from earlier that this happens before the end of the great tribulation period because the days are truncated for the elect showing that they don't go through as many as the un-elect, and it seems the only way they could be truncated is by Jesus gathering the elect to His self so that at his physical return, we can ride on horses with Him as we will see in Revelation 19.

"But wait," you may be saying, "verse 30 says they will see the Son of man coming on the clouds of heaven. I though the sign was different than the coming of Jesus." It is difficult when Scripture is intertwined to keep a linear conversation. Here, Mt 24 and Mt 25 contrast one another. We could wait till Mt 25 to discuss this, but it seems to discuss it now is better.

In Matthew 25:31-32 we read the following:

> *31 When the Son of man shall come in his glory, and all the holy angels with him, then shall he sit upon the throne of his glory: 32 And before him shall be gathered all nations: and he shall separate them one from another, as a shepherd divideth [his] sheep from the goats:*

Matthew 25:31 explains that the Son of man will come in His glory, and all the holy angels with him at which point He will ascend His throne. This is what immediately before the millennial reign of Jesus, the time in history where Jesus will rule the earth for 1,000 years as the only King of Kings and Lord of Lords. You'll note here that Scripture states "and all the holy angels with him." The word "angels" in the Greek[40] can also mean envoys or messengers. It is my considered opinion that this use in Mt 25:31 means all the hosts of heaven, angels and resurrected

---

[40] ἄγγελος pronounced as ang'-el-os (Strongs G32) which means "a messenger, envoy, one who is sent, an angel, a messenger from God."

saints, because this understanding would agree with Revelation 19. Consider this Scripture from Matthew 25 in parallel with some Scripture from Revelation 19:

| Mt 25:31-32 | Rev 19:11-14; 20:11-12 |
|---|---|
| [31]When the Son of man shall come in his glory, | [19:11]And I saw heaven opened, and behold a white horse; and he that sat upon him [was] called Faithful and True, and in righteousness he doth judge and make war. [12]His eyes [were] as a flame of fire, and on his head [were] many crowns; and he had a name written, that no man knew, but he himself. [13]And he [was] clothed with a vesture dipped in blood: and his name is called The Word of God. |
| [31]...and all the holy angels with him | [19:14]And the armies [which were] in heaven followed him upon white horses, clothed in fine linen, white and clean. |
| [31]...then shall he sit upon the throne of his glory | [20:11]And I saw a great white throne, and him that sat on it, from whose face the earth and the heaven fled away; and there was found no place for them. |
| [32]And before him shall be gathered all nations | [20:12]And I saw the dead, small and great, stand before God... [13]And the sea gave up the dead which were in it; and death and hell delivered up the dead which were in them: |
| [32]...and he shall separate them one from another, as a shepherd divideth [his] sheep from the goats[41] | [12]...and the books were opened: and another book was opened, which is [the book] of life: and the dead were judged out of those things which were written in the books, according to their works. |

---

[41] Mt 25:31-46 explains that the sheep and goats are known by their works: sheep are those who acted gracefully and benevolently toward the least of mankind; goats are those who did not.

110

You can see from these parallel accounts that Mt 25 and Rev 19 appear to match one another and if this is the case, then when the "Son of man shall come in his glory" is different from the appearance of the sign of the Son of man in Mt 24. Just to further illustrate this point, here is a comparison between the two that shows the similarities and differences.

| Mt 24:30-31 "the sign" | Mt 25:31-32,46 "the coming" |
|---|---|
| A sign appears of Jesus in the clouds | Jesus himself returns on a horse |
| All tribes of the earth mourn (for fear of His *soon* wrath—Rev 6) | Jesus ascends the throne as King to execute judgment and wrath |
| Only the elect saints are gathered | All nations are gathered |
| Jesus is seen alone | Jesus is seen with his envoys |
| Angels given tasks to fulfill – gather elect from four winds and all of heaven | No tasks given the angels |
| Great sound of a trumpet heralds the event | No defining sounds |
| No judgment listed | Final judgment listed (v. 46) |

As you can see when you compare the events immediately describing Mt 24's sign of the Son of man against Mt 25's Son of man coming in glory, there are some substantial differences. Now, in absolute transparency, there is one thing we don't know and that we can only guess so far; and that is the time span between *the sign of the Son of man* and *the coming of the Son of man in His glory*; but there is one *major* take away point here: Mt 24 and Jesus' conversation are making a defined point. Let's reread the verse before making it:

> *36But of that day and hour knoweth no [man], no, not the angels of heaven, but my Father only.*

This verse is discussing the sign of the Son of man only. The sign is different than the coming and they are separated by at least a small amount of time, and potentially as much as 3½ years depending on the outcome of the discussion "unless the Lord had shortened those days..." as well as a few other defining points which I will cover in the following paragraphs.

## What Scripture Says Without Saying It

We now have three unknown time periods: 1) the expanse of time from the re-starting of the tamid until it stops at the revealing of the abomination of desolation; 2) the expanse of time between the revealing of the abomination of desolation and the gathering of the elect to Jesus; and 3) the expanse of time from the gathering of the elect to Jesus' final glorious return with all the elect by His side as His entourage. The fact that the tribes of the earth mourn at the sign of the Son of man (Mt 24:30) means that they have time to express their emotion, to make plans and to execute them. We see at the 6th seal that the kings of the earth "hid themselves in the dens and rocks of the mountains" because they were seemingly afraid of impending judgment, which when compared to Mt 24 was the sign of the Son of man. In Mt 24 (referencing Rev 6) people mourn, hiding in the dens and in the rocks of the mountains, but in Mt 25 (referencing Rev 19) we see that there are no mountains because they've all been collapsed to the ground in Rev. 16:20 where we see that "the mountains were not found."

The point that I'm making here is that between the appearing of *the sign of the Son* and the appearing of *the Son in power*, there has to be enough time for the full destruction of the mountains as well as for the kings of the earth to react, mourn and hide.  Now, while this could happen in hours, it seems more believable given the unfolding events of the last days that these will happen over a matter of days, weeks or possibly months.  We will visit this topic in detail as we enter Daniel, but I believe that Scripture explains that *the sign of the appearing of the Son of man* and *the return of the Son of man in glory* are very close to each other at the end of the last days, and the word "meet" is why.

## We Shall *Meet* the Lord in the Air—Then What?

This is as good a time as ever to explain another reason why I believe the two events of *the sign of Jesus* and *the coming of Jesus in power and great glory* are very closely related by days or weeks instead of months or years.  It revolves around Scripture that discusses our meeting the Lord in the air and remaining with Him forever.  Let's read it together to remind ourselves what 1Thes 4:15-18 states:

> *15For this we say unto you by the word of the Lord, that we which are alive [and] remain unto the coming of the Lord shall not prevent them which are asleep. 16For the Lord himself shall descend from heaven with a shout, with the voice of the archangel, and with the trump of God: and the dead in Christ shall rise first: 17Then we which are alive [and] remain shall be caught up together with them in the clouds, to meet the Lord in the air: and so shall we ever be with the Lord. 18Wherefore comfort one another with these words.*

This section of Scripture gives us great context for what will happen when Jesus comes to gather the elect.  Inside these verses, I want to focus on verse 17. We know the gathering of the elect will happen and we likely know all the main points by heart: Jesus will descend with a shout and the trump of God; the dead rise first; the elect are instantaneously changed into resurrected bodies; the elect meet Jesus in the clouds; and they are forever with Jesus. The specific word of interest here is the word "meet." We want Scripture to interpret scripture, so let's see how this word is used other places. First off, the word *meet* appears 23 times in the New Testament, but there is more than one word in Greek translated as *meet* in English. The Greek word for *meet*[42] in 1Thes 4:16-17 is only used four times in the New Testament, so it won't be hard to evaluate.

## Ten Virgins Meet the Bridegroom

The parable of the ten virgins houses our target word two times. Let's read the parable and make a few observations about how the word *meet* is used. Here is the parable:

> [1]*Then shall the kingdom of heaven be likened unto ten virgins, which took their lamps, and went forth to meet the bridegroom.* [2]*And five of them were wise, and five [were] foolish.* [3]*They that [were] foolish took their lamps, and took no oil with them:* [4]*But the wise took oil in their vessels with their lamps.* [5]*While the bridegroom tarried, they all slumbered and slept.* [6]*And at midnight there was a cry made, Behold, the bridegroom cometh; go ye out to meet him.* [7]*Then all those virgins arose, and trimmed their lamps.* [8]*And the foolish said unto the wise, Give us of your oil; for our lamps are gone out.* [9]*But the wise answered, saying, [Not so]; lest there be not enough for us and you: but go ye rather to them that sell, and buy for yourselves.* [10]*And while they went to buy, the*

---

[42] ἀπάντησις pronounced as ap-an'-tay-sis (Strongs G529)

*bridegroom came; and they that were ready went in with him to the marriage: and the door was shut. [11]Afterward came also the other virgins, saying, Lord, Lord, open to us. [12]But he answered and said, Verily I say unto you, I know you not. [13]Watch therefore, for ye know neither the day nor the hour wherein the Son of man cometh.*

In wireframe format, here is the record of events. There was a bridegroom and ten virgins → the bridegroom goes away → five of the virgins were wise and five foolish → the five wise brought extra oil for their lamps because they didn't know when the bridegroom was coming → all slumbered and slept → the cry happened at midnight, "the bridegroom cometh, go ye out to meet him" → virgins get up → five wise go into the wedding banquet → the rest are never allowed in.

The topic here is the word *meet* and it's found at the beginning and is nestled in the middle of the parable. Here, it represents the action the virgins experience in relationship to the bridegroom. The word *meet* is a shared action between the bridegroom and the virgins. The account is directed from the vantage point of the bridegroom as the subject and the virgins being the supporting actors and objects of the teaching. In other words, it is the virgins who go to meet the bridegroom and not the other way around. Why? Because the bridegroom is the important one and the virgins are there solely to serve him in his wedding preparations. The bridegroom is not servant to the virgins: it is the bridegroom's wedding! This makes the bridegroom the most important player in this parable. We will interact with this parable and its other meanings a bit later, but for now, our sole focus is figuring out what specific value is carried by the word *meet*.

So, what happens when the virgins *meet* the bridegroom? Let's see the verses again:

> *Mt 25:6,10And at midnight there was a cry made, Behold, the bridegroom cometh; go ye out to meet him...the bridegroom came; and they that were ready went in with him to the marriage: and the door was shut.*

The virgins meet the bridegroom as he's already on his way to the wedding; the bridegroom and the virgins who are prepared go into the wedding and the door is shut behind them. In wireframe format: bridegroom headed toward the wedding → cry goes out at midnight "go meet the bridegroom" → virgins meet the bridegroom on his way to the wedding → they join the bridegroom in his journey → bridegroom and five wise virgins go into the wedding.

### Brothers from Rome Meet Paul

Now, let's look at the next reference. It happens to be in Acts 28 and it speaks of the apostle Paul. Let me give you some background before we jump into the actual Scripture itself. Paul is at Caesarea with a Roman ruler named Porcius Festus when King Agrippa and his wife Bernice arrive to visit Porcius Festus. They learn of Paul who then tells all of them the gospel of Jesus. Paul is assaulted by Jewish leaders who demand that he be brought to trial in Jerusalem, but Paul, being a Roman citizen as well as a Jew, appeals to Caesar and is granted his request. We pick up the account in Acts 28. Paul has been travelling for several months already; has gone through storms, shipwreck, floating on driftwood for days in the ocean, a venomous snake bite and now is on dry land walking to Rome to appear before Nero Caesar – the demented, demoniac who dips Christians in oil and burns them at night to light his courtyards.

We pick up the account in Acts 28:11 and journey with Paul into verse 15.

> [11]*And after three months we departed in a ship of Alexandria, which had wintered in the isle, whose sign was Castor and Pollux.* [12]*And landing at Syracuse, we tarried [there] three days.* [13]*And from thence we fetched a compass, and came to Rhegium: and after one day the south wind blew, and we came the next day to Puteoli:* [14]*Where we found brethren, and were desired to tarry with them seven days: and so we went toward Rome.* [15]*And from thence, when the brethren heard of us, they came to meet us as far as Appii forum, and The three taverns: whom when Paul saw, he thanked God, and took courage.* [16]*And when we came to Rome, the centurion delivered the prisoners to the captain of the guard: but Paul was suffered to dwell by himself with a soldier that kept him.*

What do we see here? We see Paul, the great apostle of the church, travelling his way to Rome to stand trial in front of Nero Caesar. Look at verse 15 specifically: "…And from thence [Rome], when the brethren heard of us, they came to meet us [from Rome] as far as Appii forum, and The three taverns…." So, Paul is coming from Caesarea to Rome. Brothers in Rome hear about Paul coming and they travel toward him on the route as far as Appii Forum and The three taverns, which appears to be roughly 33 miles or a four to five day's journey on foot. Who made the effort to meet whom? Paul is the subject. The brothers are the object. The brothers travelled to meet Paul. Paul was going to Rome whether the brothers met him or not. The brothers from Rome meet Paul at Appii Forum and The three taverns and they encourage him. Then, verse 16 says, "And when we came to Rome...." So, they met Paul and then walked with him back to Rome. Now, just like before, let's look at this in wireframe format: Paul headed to Rome → brothers in Rome hear Paul is coming → brothers in Rome journey to meet Paul as he's still a distance from Rome → they join Paul for an indeterminate amount of time → Paul and the brothers continue to Rome.

What facts are common to each account? Both Mt 25 and Acts 28 follow the same pattern:

- Someone of importance is on a journey to a pre-defined destination (bridegroom and Paul);
- people associated to the important person hear he is coming ("at midnight the cry went out", "when the brothers from Rome heard about Paul");
- the person of importance is intersected by a supporting cast (virgins for the bridegroom and brothers from Rome for Paul); and
- those people join the person of importance on their journey to usher him to his intended and already determined location (the wedding feast and Rome).

### The Elect Meet Jesus

Now that we have the pattern that Scripture defines for use of this word, let's see how we apply this understanding to 1Thes 4:15-18. As a refresher, here are the verses.

*<sup>15</sup>For this we say unto you by the word of the Lord, that we which are alive [and] remain unto the coming of the Lord shall not prevent them which are asleep. <sup>16</sup>For the Lord himself shall descend from heaven with a shout, with the voice of the archangel, and with the trump of God: and the dead in Christ shall rise first: <sup>17</sup>Then we which are alive [and] remain shall be caught up together with them in the clouds, to meet the Lord in the air: and so shall we ever be with the Lord. <sup>18</sup>Wherefore comfort one another with these words.*

Let's fill in the blanks of the pattern we uncovered from the bridegroom and Paul:

- Who is the person of importance in 1Thes 4:15-18? Jesus.
- Where is Jesus headed? To the earth from heaven.
- Who are the supporting cast? Those who are alive and remain unto the coming of the Lord and those who have died before.
- Where does the supporting cast usher Jesus? To the earth.

Do you see the interesting part of this account? It all has to do with a very specific word in the Greek language that is only used four times in the New Testament. The word is ἀπάντησις[43] pronounced as ap-an'-tay-sis and it means "the greeting of a newly arriving dignitary." This specific word means that **the purpose of the supporting cast is always to properly intersect the person of importance and to usher him to his intended destination**. In the case of the virgins,

---

[43] ἀπάντησις pronounced ap-an'-tay-sis (Strongs G529)

they met the bridegroom and ushered him into the wedding. In the case of Paul, the brothers from Rome met him and ushered him to Rome. In the case of the elect, they meet Jesus in the air, and usher him to the Earth where He rules and reigns from that point forward!

Do you see how Scripture uses this word? The amount of time from the meeting to the final destination does not appear intended to include years of inactivity or interlude. The meeting purpose is to greet and usher the dignitary to their destination. Remember, the person of importance sets the target location and purpose; those greeting the person of importance are not decision makers in the journey, only supporting players. This is one further reason, perhaps even the strongest reason, why I believe it's very unlikely that the catching away of the elect will happen early in the days of the beast-man's kingdom. That idea appears to conflict with the understanding and use of this very specific Greek word for *meet*.

## Pulling it Together (Mt 24:36)

It seems to me, from everything I can see, that Jesus will come toward the earth from Heaven, the world will see the sign of His coming and respond in mourning and fear, hiding in dens and caves that *still exist at the time* because the mountains have not yet been demolished[44]; the elect will be

---

[44] This is an important point because when Jesus returns physically in power to the earth in Revelation 19, the mountains have just been leveled and all the islands removed in Revelation 17 and if the sign of the Son and the coming of the Son in glory were the same event, there would be no mountains and dens in which to hide. This means there must be some difference in time to allow for the destruction of the mountains between the sign of the Son and the coming of the Son.

caught up to meet Jesus in the clouds and then the elect will turn around and usher Him to the earth as the person of importance who has already established the traveling direction and destination. And while I cannot definitively state the length of time between the elect meeting Jesus in the air and His return to earth, I can say that in the case of the bridegroom and Paul, it appears nearly immediate for the bridegroom and it was mere days for Paul. From these vantage points, as we let Scripture interpret scripture, the elect being caught into the heavens and then waiting multiple years before Jesus physical return to earth doesn't appear supported. There appears to be a much stronger and compelling presence of Scripture to believe the turnaround of the elect with Jesus, as He comes to the earth, will be short, making the sign of Jesus coming very close to his physical return to rule and reign over the earth.

# Noah Days, the Goodman, Tares and a Servant

As we step into Matthew 24:36-44, we begin to move out of the sign of the Son of man and into the coming of the Son at His final return. Let's read it together and then begin to dissect it.

*³⁶But of that day and hour knoweth no [man], no, not the angels of heaven, but my Father only. ³⁷But as the days of Noe [were], so shall also the coming of the Son of man be. ³⁸For as in the days that were before the flood they were eating and drinking, marrying and giving in marriage, until the day that Noe entered into the ark, ³⁹And knew not until the flood came, and took them all away; so shall also the coming of the Son of man be. ⁴⁰Then shall two be in the field; the one shall be taken, and the other left. ⁴¹Two [women shall be] grinding at the mill; the one shall be taken, and the other left. ⁴²Watch therefore: for ye know not what hour your Lord doth come.*

*43But know this, that if the goodman of the house had known in what watch the thief would come, he would have watched, and would not have suffered his house to be broken up. 44Therefore be ye also ready: for in such an hour as ye think not the Son of man cometh.*

We begin with the understanding that no angel, no man and not even Jesus knows when the elect will be gathered to meet Him and when the sign of His coming is made visible to the world. It will be a complete surprise to everyone, including Jesus Himself (Mk 13:32). From the vantage point of the veiled appearing, Jesus discusses His coming and identifies that it will be like the days of Noah. Note how quickly we move from the sign of Jesus' appearing to His physical return? This is one more reason I believe the time between the catching away of the elect is very close to the physical return of Jesus.

## Parable of the Days of Noah (Mt 24:36-42)

In Mt 24:36-42, Jesus states that the world, at his return, will be just as when Noah and his family entered the ark: everyone was eating, drinking, marrying and giving in marriage. No one had any idea of the impending doom until the flood came and took them all away. The first question we must answer is, who are "them" who were all taken away? Is it Noah and his family? Or is it the lost world who was drowned in the deluge? Let's use some deductive reasoning to figure it out. We'll do it in comparative form. Let's put Noah and his family on the left and the lost world on the right. In case you don't know the historical account of Noah, you can read it in Genesis 6:5-8:22.

| Noah | Not Noah |
|---|---|
| Built ark in preparation | Didn't build ark in preparation |
| Family in the ark | No one in the ark |
| Knew what he was doing because of God's instruction | Were not concerned as none built their own ark |
| Knew God was sending a flood because God told him | Had no idea God was sending a flood because they all drowned (Gen 7:21-23) |
| Had faith he would float away in safety | Were unconcerned for safety as they were all destroyed (Gen 7:21-23) |

When you consider the account, who appears to have known and taken seriously that they would be taken away in the flood and who did not know or take seriously that they would be taken away in the flood? Matthew 24:39 records:

> *[39]And knew not until the flood came, and took them all away; so shall also the coming of the Son of man be.*

The only people who did not know or take seriously that they were being taken away in the flood were the non-Noah people: everyone who was *not* Noah's family. "But are you sure?" you may be thinking. Let's look at another observation in Scripture to underscore this point. In Matthew 24:38 Jesus states:

> *[38]For as in the days that were before the flood they were eating and drinking, marrying and giving in marriage, until the day that Noe entered into the ark....*

Certainly, Noah and his family were eating and drinking up to the day they entered the ark, as was the rest of the world, but what does "giving in marriage" mean? This

Greek word[45] is used five other times in the New Testament and most often means the giving of a daughter in marriage. Luke's gospel makes this observation even more clear in his writing of the account where he underscores the difference between "married wives" and "given in marriage" in Luke 17:27:

> *[27]They did eat, they drank, they married wives, they were given in marriage, until the day that Noe entered into the ark, and the flood came, and destroyed them all.*

This concept of being "given in marriage" cannot apply to Noah because Noah never had any daughters. We know this because Genesis 7:1 states:

> *[1]And the LORD said unto Noah, Come thou and all thy house into the ark; for thee have I seen righteous before me in this generation.*

As there were no daughters of Noah who entered the Ark, and since God's promise was to Noah's household, we observe He must have had none. The skeptic may respond with, "Well, if Noah had daughters and they were married, they wouldn't be part of his house anymore." The fallacy of this argument, however, suggests that Noah's sons *were still part of his house* even though *they were* already married. Still, we can allow for the sons to be saved and the daughters destroyed if we must as it's still a possibility. Even with this, it remains that the only ones who didn't know when the flood would come were the non-Noah people as God specifically tells Noah, "it will rain in seven days" (Gen 7:4).

---

[45] ἐκγαμίζω pronounced as ek-gam-id'-zo (Strongs G1547)

Some may reply, "But Noah was delivered from judgment. Isn't God's heart to save the elect from wrath?" Let's consider the idea that Noah was delivered from all the horrible atrocities of the flood through his escape on the ark. Let's be circumspect about Noah's situation. This was not paradise for Noah. Consider what he had to endure as the wrath of God was poured out upon the earth: the narrative wasn't as simple as "Noah entered the ark, the flood came and destroyed mankind, Noah left the ark and lived happily ever after." Here is what Noah endured.

- Noah spent upwards of 100 years building the ark that was ~500 feet long, ~50 feet wide and three stories tall without the use of hydraulics or cranes, having to carry everything, drill every hole by hand, cut every board by hand, etc., etc., and etcetera.

- Noah entered the boat with his sons and daughters-in-law and lived *only* with the same seven people for a year in a completely enclosed vessel with thousands of animals, creeping things and birds.

- God brought the animals to Noah that needed to live on the Ark, seven pairs of animals that could be eaten and one pairs of those that could not, male and female and Noah was responsible for their placement and care (Gen 7:2).

- Noah was personally responsible to gather all necessary food to feed all the animals and all members of his family in the ark for a year— Noah gathered and stored the food, not God (Gen 6:21).

- Noah started building the ark somewhere between his 500th and 600th birthday.
- Noah entered when he was 600 years, two months and 17 days old (Gen 7:11) and it rained 40 days while he and all these family and animals were in a wooden enclosure with only one wooden window (no glass) through which they likely ejected animal feces every day.
- The ark was floating in water until the seventh month and the 17th day—they floated five months in the ark with whatever waves and ocean motions existed.
- A year from the day they entered the ark, in the second month and on the 20th day (Gen 8:14) the land was dry, and Noah and his family could finally disembark—it had been one year and three days they were living in the ark with no glass windows and the beautiful aroma of animal odors, urine, feces and everything else that they had to eject from the ark daily.
- Their entire lives were spent for a year, living in a wooden container, caring for animals and each other. Day and night, day after day for a year! Not a week, a year!
- Noah exited the ark and likely had to first create larger implements with which to farm.
- Noah had to break up the ground, till the ground, and prepare the ground to receive seed since the flood had leveled all farming ground and new grass, weeds and thorns had been growing.

- Noah had to plant crops and vineyards (Gen 9:20) all over again, had to build houses, build fences and assumably dig water wells again.
- Noah had to continue raising animals to build up flocks and herds for food and clothing.

Do you get the idea here? Now, who experienced tribulation and who experienced wrath? Did the people in Noah's account experience tribulation or wrath? Did Noah and his family experience tribulation or wrath? Some fall prey to the fallacy that because Noah was protected from God's wrath he was also protected from tribulation. We cannot lump tribulation and wrath together as a single experience. I would submit to you that while Noah did not die in God's wrath through the flood, Noah still went through the flood, protected by God, but observably through great tribulation.

If you may yet be skeptical about the interpretation of the parable of Noah, you should wrestle with why? Is it because the Scripture says something I'm not saying or because you are defending a fear? Either way, shelf your thought and keep reading.

Scripture seems to present that Mt 24:39 is all non-Noah individuals, and I believe we can summarize the Noah experience in the following phrase:

*Noah and his family knew the flood was coming and were preparing up to 120 years before[46]; everyone else did not prepare and were taken away.*

---

[46] Genesis 6:3 states God's warning at the 120-year mark.

From this learning, let's continue evaluating the rest of this section to see what we can find. Let's re-read the next few verses:

*37But as the days of Noe [were], so shall also the coming of the Son of man be...40Then shall two be in the field; the one shall be taken, and the other left. 41Two [women shall be] grinding at the mill; the one shall be taken, and the other left. 42Watch therefore: for ye know not what hour your Lord doth come.*

The template for the coming of Jesus is the days of Noah. Who was taken away in the days of Noah? The ones who knew not that the flood was coming. Who knew not the flood was coming? The non-Noah people who did not hear God and did not prepare. So here, when we read verses 40-42, what do we see? Two people in each circumstance where one is taken, and the other is not taken. In Noah's experience, who was taken? The wicked. Therefore, this Scripture in Matthew cannot be talking about the catching away of the elect as some believe. This is talking about some type of judgment. There are two people and one of the two is taken away to judgment. Remember, in the Noah experience, those who were taken away were those who did not know. Recall these verses?

*38For as in the days that were before the flood they were eating and drinking, marrying and giving in marriage, until the day that Noe entered into the ark, 39And knew not until the flood came, and took them all away; so shall also the coming of the Son of man be.*

Noah entered the ark. The people did not. Noah knew that God was sending a flood. The people, by observation of Scripture, did not know that God was sending a flood. Noah knew and cared. The people appeared to be fully unaware of the fact that a flood was coming until it was too late, even though Noah spent up to 100 years building an ark in front of their eyes. This is the pattern for the end times. Those individuals taken in Mt 24:38-39 will be those who were not aware they needed to do something and because they were oblivious to their need to prepare or act, they will be taken away.

Finally, Jesus ends with Matthew 24:42:

> *⁴²Watch therefore: for ye know not what hour your Lord doth come.*

If we allow Scripture to interpret Scripture, where in Scripture can we find an example of the end times, where Jesus destroys the wicked and leaves the righteous? This section of Mt 24:36-40, which we are now reading, suggests that at the coming of the Son, wicked people will be taken away and the righteous will not which seems backward when considering the gathering of the elect. Do we have any other examples in Scripture where the wicked are taken and the righteous left behind? What about Jesus' parable of the tares?

## Parable of the Tares

Let's read this parable out of Matthew 13 to see if it could apply:

> *²⁴Another parable put he forth unto them, saying, The kingdom of heaven is likened unto a man which sowed good seed in his field: ²⁵But while men slept,*

*his enemy came and sowed tares* [thistles/thorns] *among the wheat, and went his way. ²⁶But when the blade was sprung up, and brought forth fruit, then appeared the tares also. ²⁷So the servants of the householder came and said unto him, Sir, didst not thou sow good seed in thy field? from whence then hath it tares? ²⁸He said unto them, An enemy hath done this. The servants said unto him, Wilt thou then that we go and gather them up? ²⁹But he said, Nay; lest while ye gather up the tares, ye root up also the wheat with them. ³⁰Let both grow together until the harvest: and in the time of harvest I will say to the reapers, Gather ye together first the tares, and bind them in bundles to burn them: but gather the wheat into my barn.*

In this parable, Jesus identifies the kingdom of heaven with an effort to remove the tares at the harvest, then to gather in the wheat. This idea matches Jesus words about "as in the days of Noah." What happened in the days of Noah? The thorns (the wicked) were destroyed, and the wheat (Noah and his family) were gathered in the barn (the ark). It seems to me that verse 42 is the requisite response in all cases:

*⁴²Watch therefore: for ye know not what hour your Lord doth come.*

Another aspect of this verse that catches my attention is the phrase "your Lord doth come." These are people under the Lordship of Jesus. Could this mean all humanity? Possibly because Jesus is "King of kings and Lord of lords" (Rev 17:14, 19:16); but as we will see, there is a warning and potential judgment for anyone who claims to be a

131

follower of Jesus in word but does not pursue Him in their deeds. In either case, these two groups share one thing in common: these are people whose Lord is Jesus and who are not prepared at His coming; they are removed from His kingdom so that only the good remain. It does not appear that Scripture supports the parable of Noah as representing the gathering of the elect to Jesus at his appearing; rather, it appears to reflect the removal of the wicked at Jesus' appearing instead.

## Parable of the Goodman (Mt 24:43-44)

Consider the next few verses of Jesus' words in Mt 24:43-44:

> *[43]But know this, that if the goodman of the house had known in what watch the thief would come, he would have watched, and would not have suffered his house to be broken up. [44]Therefore be ye also ready: for in such an hour as ye think not the Son of man cometh.*

Once again, the topic is *being prepared.* The goodman[47] is not prepared! Jesus says,

> *[43]But know this, that **if the goodman of the house had known** [emphasis added]*

Jesus says "if" which means the goodman *didn't know* when the thief was coming and that the goodman *wasn't* prepared to defend his home. If the goodman had inside information that the thief was coming at 1AM, Jesus is saying he would have been awake, armed and ready to defend! But even the goodman did not have any idea when

---

[47] The term "goodman" means "master" or "caretaker" and has nothing to do with being good or bad.

the thief was coming. Jesus is saying, the only way to prepare for the unknown time of His return is to always *be ready*. Verse 44 only underscores this point:

> *44Therefore be ye also ready: for in such an hour as ye think not the Son of man cometh.*

## Parable of the Faithful/Unfaithful Servant (Mt 24:45-51)

To help us process the idea of being always ready, Jesus introduces the parable of the faithful and unfaithful servant in verses 45-51. Let's read the scriptures first and then unpack them:

> *45Who then is a faithful and wise servant, whom his lord hath made ruler over his household, to give them meat in due season? 46Blessed [is] that servant, whom his lord when he cometh shall find so doing. 47Verily I say unto you, That he shall make him ruler over all his goods. 48But and if that evil servant shall say in his heart, My lord delayeth his coming; 49And shall begin to smite [his] fellowservants, and to eat and drink with the drunken; 50The lord of that servant shall come in a day when he looketh not for [him], and in an hour that he is not aware of, 51And shall cut him asunder, and appoint [him] his portion with the hypocrites: there shall be weeping and gnashing of teeth.*

Here we have the representation of a faithful and wise servant (v. 45) and the representation of an evil servant (v. 48). These are the one and same individual, given a circumstance over which to care: this person is made the ruler over the master's house while the master is away. The servant has one responsibility: to give the master's household meat in due season. One person, one job, two scenarios, two outcomes. In the first outcome, the person is called "faithful and wise"; in the second outcome, the person is called "evil." What was the difference?

> $^{46}$Blessed [is] that servant, whom his lord when he cometh shall find so doing...

Doing what? The answer is in the verse before:

> $^{45}$[being] ruler over his household, to give them meat in due season

The evil servant is of a different heart. The evil servant is convinced he has control over the timing of the master's return and a false sense of security in his ability to be punished as a servant. Jesus says this:

> $^{48}$But and if that evil servant shall say in his heart, My lord delayeth his coming; $^{49}$And shall begin to smite [his] fellowservants, and to eat and drink with the drunken;

Those words in verses 48 and 49 are what make the servant evil: the servant says in his heart "I've got time; I can do what I want" and then does what he wants, *knowing* his actions are not representative of the master's trust. What is the summary here? The same servant is given trust and responsibility by his master; two different scenarios play out; two different outcomes achieved. Scenario one: he does what he's supposed to and represents his master while gone and is rewarded as ruler over all his master's goods. Scenario two: he takes advantage of the master's absence, abuses his position, does what he wants with whom he wants and is punished when the master returns.

Now catch this: it is the same person who starts in the good favor of his master. In both cases, he starts as a highly favored worker with the potential of ruling over *everything* the master has. You can't start from a more trusted and favored position than to be a servant entrusted with the master's favor. These different results come out of the *same* person…not two different people…not one good person and one wicked person, but one and the same person *capable of producing good and evil.* Are you seeing that it's the same person? Let's not lose this. Verse 48 says, "But and if…." But the evil servant says in his heart; and if the evil servant says in his heart. Jesus says "but and if" meaning the one who is an evil servant *will say this in his heart* but that the servant doesn't have to respond this way, it is only *if that evil servant says in his heart.* Not only is this the same person, but even if the servant started as evil, the judgment waiting will only apply to him *if he says in his heart.* Jesus is in essence communicating, "Look humanity. Whether you start from a good heart or start from an evil heart, there is always the ability to do what I expect and what is right, and I will reward you accordingly."

Now, from this point, let's reach the conclusion. This is the same servant, trusted by the master, in a place of authority to feed his house while he is gone, with the ability to squander that opportunity, to waste it and to be found as evil when the master returns. When the master returns, is that person no longer a servant? Did they lose the position of servant before the master returned? No. When the master left, the person was a servant; when the master returns, the person is *still a servant;* and as a servant the person is now judged and what happens to the servant who is still a servant and who now gets judged? Matthew 24:50-51 tells us:

135

*[50]The lord of that servant shall come in a day when he looketh not for [him], and in an hour that he is not aware of, [51]And shall cut him asunder, and appoint [him] his portion with the hypocrites: there shall be weeping and gnashing of teeth.*

The servant, in high standing with the master when he leaves, does not do what the master wants and instead acts selfishly and at the return of the master, that servant, still a servant, is cut in two[48] and appointed his portion with hypocrites where there is weeping and gnashing of teeth. Being *cut asunder* or cut in two can only be metaphorical here because of the rest of the verse. Read it again:

*[51]And shall cut him asunder, and appoint [him] his portion with the hypocrites: there shall be weeping and gnashing of teeth.*

The evil servant is given an appointed portion and after the person is *cut asunder* they weep and gnash their teeth. If it were literal, the person could not weep or grind their teeth; this should be understood to be a severe punishment, possibly even a strong whipping. The servant isn't cast into eternal judgment, the servant is punished in the most severe way and then seems to realize he or she failed, where in absolute remorse and anguish he or she wishes they could correct their actions, but where they will not be able to change the fact that all hope of reward is forever lost, and so they will weep and grind their teeth in anguish because of the lost opportunities that will never again exist with no chance to earn an eternal reward or the favor of the master. It will be a time of absolute and deep self-assessment and

---

[48] διχοτομέω pronounced dee-khot-om-eh'-o (Strongs G1371).

regret; one of great sadness for a servant who wastes his or her time, authority, responsibility and position and can do nothing to repair that fact.

From this vantage point, it should not be hard to see why the person is called a hypocrite. The person is a servant by position, appointment, empowerment, trust and title but is not acting like a servant. The Greek word for hypocrite[49] uses the following words and phrases to explain the term: an interpreter, pretender, actor, stage player. Still a servant, not acting like a servant.

Why do you think I have hammered the point of Jesus' parable that the person judged is the same servant in both scenarios? Why did I make certain to underscore that the person is a servant at the time they are judged by the master and thrown into weeping and gnashing of teeth? It's because Scripture is plain that we are judged by our works. If a person is truly a Jesus follower, a true one of the elect, that person will hate sin, will be sorrowful when they commit sin, will want out of sin, will want to make the master glad at his return, will do whatever is necessary to represent the master while he's gone. Jesus is the master in this parable; Jesus-followers and perhaps even all of humankind is the servant. Each person has the same beginning place. The evil heart can choose what is right and to do it ("but and if"). The good heart can choose what is right and to do it. What makes the outcome good? Doing what is right. If you join me as a follower of Jesus, we cannot allow ourselves to get off track; we need to compare ourselves to Scripture to find our position, correct our attitudes and change our actions before it's too late. Don't rely on your perception of grace

---

[49] ὑποκριτής pronounced as hoop-ok-ree-tace' (Strongs G5273)

to give you a false sense of security: there is more to grace than a free ticket out of damnation, and Jesus is showing us this in the parable of the servants.

## Pulling it Together (Mt 24:36-51)

When Jesus speaks in Mt 24:36-44 about his return being like the days of Noah, he's not telling us we will be taken away unexpectedly in the gathering of the elect to Him in the clouds; He is warning us that if we don't honor Him and His kingdom and prove ourselves by our deeds, if we are not alert to the signs of our times, if we are not vigilant to keep our attention outward and watchful; honoring and obedient, then when the time comes for His return, we will be unprepared and suffer great loss. We are told to *be ready at all times* because we don't know the day or hour when He's coming, and yet, **the fact we do not know the day or hour does not mean Jesus' return will happen before anything else.**

When Jesus speaks of the servants in Mt 24:45-51, there is one servant, one assignment, two different heart attitudes, two different actions and two different outcomes. We are to be doing the master's assigned tasks faithfully, representing him as he expects to be represented without veering off. We are not to use our freedom as an occasion to sin and live a life unrepresentative of Him so that we then step into the servant judgment. We are to *be always ready* for His return, carrying out His duties faithfully.

These verses, from 36-51, prefixed with "as it was in the days of Noah" are not a representation of the blessing of the elect that happens at the coming of Jesus, but the representation of what happens at His physical return, when He comes to rule and reign for 1,000 years as King of the earth. The removal of the wicked from His kingdom happens at His physical return as described in Revelation 19. The sign of Noah is not the gathering of the elect at the sign of His coming. For us, the takeaway is simple: we must always pursue Him and we must *be ready* at every moment to see Him face to face. We must be focused and dedicated, representing Him and doing His will at every moment until He returns to find us faithful (or evil) and rewards us according to our lifestyle and deeds. Are you challenged by those words? Yep. Me too.

# Virgins, Talents, Sheep and Goats

We touched on the parable of the ten virgins earlier, but as we enter Matthew 25, this parable is now our main focus. Please remember, the chapter numbers and divisions didn't exist when Jesus was speaking. I know this is common sense to many, but we would do well to mentally adjust and remember that Matthew 24 and Matthew 25 are all the same conversation with the disciples. Jesus is rapid-firing understandings of the last days and so far, He's given them a rundown on what will happen in a sequence that matches the seals of the Revelation; He explains in bullet points what will happen up to the end of the age and then he circles back to start filling in the blanks.

The first major point He adds to fill in some detail is the appearing of the abomination of desolation. Jesus explains that this sign is key and pivotal: when you see this sign, you *must* respond or lose your life and the appearing of the abomination of desolation is what starts the time known as *the great tribulation;* during this time there will be an increase in false Christs and false prophets intending to deceive; untimely reports of Jesus coming back to the earth will circulate; much death will happen; toward the end of this time, the sun will be darkened, the moon darkened, the stars will fall from heaven and at that point the sign of the Son will appear in the heavens, visible to the entire world; the elect are gathered to Jesus in the clouds and then…Jesus begins a series of parables to focus even more intently on what is expected of humanity as we approach His physical return that happens soon after.

The first parable is that of the fig tree (Mt 24:32-35) where we learn we should know the Scripture so intently and the signs of His return so specifically that we don't need anyone to tell us our position in the end times: we are expected to know the end-times events so well that we can tell the season of the age by them.

The second parable is that of Noah (Mt 24:36-44) where we learn that there is a judgment established for people who do not live the life that Jesus expects. Just as the wicked in Noah's day were removed because they did not listen to God, did not honor God and were not prepared for the flood, so those who meet the same criteria at Jesus' return will be the recipients of judgement.

The third parable is that of the goodman of the house (Mt 24:43-44) who did not know the hour the thief would come to break up his house. Jesus says, "be ye also ready" because we don't know the hour when the thief will come. The idea is that of vigilance: stay alert and watchful listening for sounds and watching for sights that are odd or that would cue an unexpected event is approaching.

The fourth parable is that of the servant (Mt 24:45-51) who must choose to be "faithful and wise" or "evil." It is the same servant, the same empowerment by the master, the same set of responsibilities, and different outcomes for that one servant based on his actions while the master is gone. If the servant represents his master well and carries out the duties of his responsibilities, the master rewards the "faithful and wise" servant for being astute and attentive and dedicated to producing the expected fruitfulness. If the servant takes advantage of the master's absence, abuses his freedom, and lives like the ungodly, the master rewards the "evil" servant by cutting him in two (severely punishing him) and "appoint[ing] him his portion with the hypocrites: [where] there shall be weeping and gnashing of teeth." Jesus is saying: if you are a servant, you must act like it, do the work of a servant and never forget that you always represent the master in His absence—this attitude will help keep you in check and help keep your focus. It's godly fear, one where you realize the weight of expectation and rise to the occasion in anticipation that the master will reward you for your labors: always watching, always alert, always aware.

## Parable of the Ten Virgins (Mt 25:1-13)

From the springboard of these four parables, let's invest a bit into the parable of the Ten Virgins as the fifth parable and let's focus on the content rather than merely the word *meet*[50] which was our sole focus before. Here is the parable in Mt 25:1-13:

> *¹Then shall the kingdom of heaven be likened unto ten virgins, which took their lamps, and went forth to meet the bridegroom. ²And five of them were wise,*

---

[50] See the section titled We Shall Meet the Lord in the Air – Then What?

*and five [were] foolish. <sup>3</sup>They that [were] foolish* — 

*and five [were] foolish. ³They that [were] foolish took their lamps, and took no oil with them: ⁴But the wise took oil in their vessels with their lamps. ⁵While the bridegroom tarried, they all slumbered and slept.*

*⁶And at midnight there was a cry made, Behold, the bridegroom cometh; go ye out to meet him. ⁷Then all those virgins arose, and trimmed their lamps. ⁸And the foolish said unto the wise, Give us of your oil; for our lamps are gone out. ⁹But the wise answered, saying, [Not so]; lest there be not enough for us and you: but go ye rather to them that sell, and buy for yourselves. ¹⁰And while they went to buy, the bridegroom came; and they that were ready went in with him to the marriage: and the door was shut.*

*¹¹Afterward came also the other virgins, saying, Lord, Lord, open to us. ¹²But he answered and said, Verily I say unto you, I know you not.*

*¹³Watch therefore, for ye know neither the day nor the hour wherein the Son of man cometh.*

What is the first word in this parable? "Then" is the first word. Have you realized yet how many times the word *then* exists in Mt 24 and 25? Let's start with *then* so we know where we are. What is the antecedent? What is the time frame we are pointing to? When the Son of man comes (Mt 24:29-31, 36-37, 40, 46, 48, 50). These events begin with the appearance of the sign of the Son in the clouds and end with Jesus physical presence on the mount of olives[51] at His

---

[51] Zechariah 14 describes this event in detail.

return. *Then*, when Jesus is seen coming in the clouds and finally, physically returns to the earth and touches the ground with His feet, the kingdom of Heaven will be like ten virgins which took lamps and went to meet the bridegroom.

First, let's be clear that we are dealing with ten virgins: not eight virgins and two sort-of-virgins—everyone starts with the same description and the same level of purity. Second, let's also observe that all ten exist to wait on the bridegroom: not seven of them having one set of responsibilities and the other three having another set. Finally, let's recognize that the bridegroom was a long time coming and the virgins grew tired of waiting and all of them fell asleep while waiting: it wasn't that some were awake and some asleep—all were asleep. We see then that all ten have the same position of trust, responsibilities, calling and circumstances at the beginning of this parable. Sound familiar? It should, because this is the same beginning point of: Noah, the goodman protecting his house from the thief and the servant with responsibilities in the parables before this one.

What happens next? Everyone begins at the same place with the same position of trust, the same responsibilities and the same sense of calling. At what point do we divide the group into five and five?

> *3They that [were] foolish took their lamps, and took no oil with them: 4But the wise took oil in their vessels with their lamps.*

The five foolish ones took their lamps and so did the five wise ones. So, having the lamp wasn't the dividing point. The five foolish ones were those who took no oil with them: this was the dividing point between the wise and the foolish—having additional oil with them to carry them through a long waiting period. Jesus says:

> *⁷Then all those virgins arose, and trimmed their lamps.*

This means that their lamps had been burning for a while and the oil had depleted from their lamps. You see, the need to trim the wick only happens when the wick itself starts to burn and the more the wick burns, the longer the burnt end of the wick becomes. When there is oil in the lamp, the wick works like straw and as the oil in the lamp burns, the fire at the end of the wick continues to suck up oil in the wick and to burn the oil. It seems crazy, but when there is enough oil in a lamp, or enough wax in a candle to burn, the wick itself really doesn't burn much because it is the oil that burns *through* the wick. But when there is no fuel being sucked up through the wick, then what remains is a piece of cloth or fiber material that contains the residue of the oil, and the fire begins to consume the wick itself. When that happens, you must trim off the top of it because it becomes black and brittle and will create smoke and a flame that can be dangerously high as well as pollute the air with an awful smell.

I'm drilling into the wick trimming piece for a moment because it shows us how long the bridegroom tarried. These virgins came with oil in their lamps, and the lamps were lit. They burned long enough that the oil was depleted from their lamps and the wicks were now burning on their own. All of them, again, were in the same set of circumstances, but the wise had the ability to respond to the long wait and to be prepared for the bridegroom when he arrived. The wise had brought oil with them, so they filled their lamps, trimmed their wicks and were ready to go! Now all they needed was to meet the bridegroom and usher him into the wedding. The foolish were the ones who left their position, they began running through the city at midnight when no one was selling oil, trying to find oil.

Jesus is warning us: if you wait till you experience a perceived need, it will be too late; you *cannot* prepare for the return of Jesus at the time you see the sign of His coming. Did you catch that? When you perceive the sign of Jesus' appearing, there will not be enough time to get ready to meet Him. The time between the sign of His coming and His return will be too short. There will *not* be enough time to prepare when you perceive His return. When did the cry go out?

> *[6]And at midnight there was a cry made, Behold, the bridegroom cometh; go ye out to meet him.*

When it happened, there was not enough time to get prepared to meet the bridegroom and only those who had prepared beforehand were allowed into the wedding. Please note, once again, the small amount of time between meeting the bridegroom and His physical presence at the wedding.

This is the first place we get a sense of timing for the wedding of the bridegroom. In this parable, it happens at his physical return: he joins the wise virgins at the place of the wedding before the judgment of the foolish virgins. Do you see? In wireframe format, the event is this: bridegroom goes → virgins prepare as they see fit → virgins sleep → cry goes out that the bridegroom is coming → wise virgins fill their lamps while foolish run to buy oil → bridegroom arrives, and the wise virgins go with him into the wedding → foolish ones return to find the door locked and they are not allowed in. Do you see that there is a span of time between the bridegroom and five wise virgins entering the wedding and the foolish virgins trying to get in while not being allowed?

Finally, what happens? The foolish ones are told some disturbing news they were not expecting. You see the foolish ones observably thought they would be allowed into the wedding because they were virgin attendants to the bridegroom. They thought their position as virgin attendants was enough, but was it?

> [11]*Afterward came also the other virgins, saying, Lord, Lord, open to us.* [12]*But he answered and said, Verily I say unto you, I know you not.*

The foolish virgins thought that they would be allowed entrance no matter what, that they were in charge, that they were important enough because they were virgin attendants of the bridegroom, that no matter what they did or how they were prepared they would be allowed in because of who they were; but, what we see is that because they were not prepared at the bridegrooms return, despite their status and position and calling, they were refused access to the wedding. It was not their position or status or calling that gave them access to the wedding with the bridegroom, that was just the invitation to succeed. What allowed them access was the invitation of the bridegroom *plus* their preparation, their effort to maintain vigilance, their attitude that the bridegroom's return was their focus, and that it was their responsibility to wait on him and to minister to him that opened the door for them to enjoy the wedding with the bridegroom. Those who did not take the unknown length and timing of his return seriously enough to do what they needed in preparation to always be ready were told, "I know you not."

Question: Who do the virgins represent in this parable? Who do the five wise virgins represent? Who do the five foolish virgins represent? Do you have your answers? Are you sure? Now, who is the bride in the parable? Interestingly, Jesus never speaks of the bride. File that away for later.

---

**Prophecy Watch**: Failing to constantly stay prepared for Jesus' return will cost us entry into His wedding celebration and earn the reply "I do not know you" from Jesus Himself.

---

Do you think that merely because you are a Jesus-follower you're entitled to entry into the wedding of Jesus? This Scripture would beg to disagree with you. Being a Jesus-follower is not enough to enjoy the wedding, you must also be prepared, vigilant and continually watching for Him and His return according to this parable.

## Parable of the Talents (Mt 25:14-30)

Jesus departs His teaching of the virgins, which we might summarize as: be ready, be prepared, plan and watch, and he transitions into a parable talking about three servants. Let's read it and then we'll unpack it as we did the virgins. This parable is quite long, but don't speed through it. I'll include it here in its entirety from Mt 25:14-30:

> *14For [the kingdom of heaven is] as a man travelling into a far country, [who] called his own servants, and delivered unto them his goods. 15And unto one he gave five talents, to another two, and to another one; to every man according to his several ability; and straightway took his journey. 16Then he that had*

received the five talents went and traded with the same, and made [them] other five talents. <sup>17</sup>And likewise he that [had received] two, he also gained other two. <sup>18</sup>But he that had received one went and digged in the earth, and hid his lord's money. <sup>19</sup>After a long time the lord of those servants cometh, and reckoneth with them.

<sup>20</sup>And so he that had received five talents came and brought other five talents, saying, Lord, thou deliveredst unto me five talents: behold, I have gained beside them five talents more. <sup>21</sup>His lord said unto him, Well done, [thou] good and faithful servant: thou hast been faithful over a few things, I will make thee ruler over many things: enter thou into the joy of thy lord. <sup>22</sup>He also that had received two talents came and said, Lord, thou deliveredst unto me two talents: behold, I have gained two other talents beside them. <sup>23</sup>His lord said unto him, Well done, good and faithful servant; thou hast been faithful over a few things, I will make thee ruler over many things: enter thou into the joy of thy lord.

<sup>24</sup>Then he which had received the one talent came and said, Lord, I knew thee that thou art an hard man, reaping where thou hast not sown, and gathering where thou hast not strawed: <sup>25</sup>And I was afraid, and went and hid thy talent in the earth: lo, [there] thou hast [that is] thine.

<sup>26</sup>His lord answered and said unto him, [Thou] wicked and slothful servant, thou knewest that I reap where I sowed not, and gather where I have not strawed: <sup>27</sup>Thou oughtest therefore to have put my

*money to the exchangers, and [then] at my coming I should have received mine own with usury. ²⁸Take therefore the talent from him, and give [it] unto him which hath ten talents.*

*²⁹For unto every one that hath shall be given, and he shall have abundance: but from him that hath not shall be taken away even that which he hath. ³⁰And cast ye the unprofitable servant into outer darkness: there shall be weeping and gnashing of teeth.*

As we enter this parable, we have a man travelling to a far country. Why is the word "far" important? Because it communicates that he can't just come back when he wants. There were no jets in Jesus's day. That understanding may be obvious but let me explain. When I started writing this book, I knew it would take months of work, but each day, I whittled down another piece of it. Week after week has gone by and still, I'm working on it. I can't simply "get done" with the book because I want to; it takes time to write, re-write, re-write, re-write, edit and format.

The same thing is true about a personal characteristic for which I'm known. I'm a bearded man. For three and a half years, I've been growing my beard. As I sit here and write this sentence, my beard goes down to my waist: if I shave it off today, I can't just grow it back in a month, because the only way it grows is over time. If I shave off a 3½-year beard, I will have to wait *another* 3½ years to return where I started.

With these illustrations in mind, consider travel in Jesus' day. Travel happened on foot, donkey or possibly by horse for some individuals. A hard day of walking at 2.5 miles per hour, because there were no paved roads, would have given you perhaps 10-12 miles in one day, and more likely eight. To go 30 miles would have taken four or five days with rest breaks and the unexpected events that go along with it. To make a 100-mile journey, would perhaps be 15-20 days depending on weather. If it rained, you could add days because you couldn't walk. Get the idea? There is no way the master could just "return" when he wanted to. If it took him 15 days to get somewhere, it would take another 15 to get back.

Jesus is driving home a point here: the master would be gone, it was a sure thing, and there was no way he could get back early, even if he wanted to. The servants know this fact. Now, let's keep going.

The traveling man calls his own three servants and gives them money, figuratively $5,000, $2,000 and $1,000 according to the level of trust he has in each person's abilities. Two of the servants used the money and doubled it. One of the servants hid the money so he could give it back. Verse 19 confirms the master was gone quite a while because Jesus states "after a long time" the master returns and asks about the money entrusted to each. Two of them are applauded and one of them is rebuked. This is where we want to focus.

To begin, we must understand that just like the other parables, there is equality when we start, but with one twist here. They are all servants, they all have the same master, they are all being trusted to invest the money given to them, they all experience the same delay of the master's return, but it's more than that. *The master here expects the servants to know and trust him and his expectations accurately, to operate from the trust he's invested in them, just as he gives them an amount equal to that trust.* We cannot move forward without seeing this. The master expects them to know he wants them to invest the money, he expects them to know he is interested in gain, he wants them to trust him and his belief in them to produce outcomes, whatever they may be. The servant's ability to fulfill the master's desire then makes the master happy and interested in trusting the servants even more with his kingdom. Do you see this?

Next, look at the reward and the judgment. Those servants who *knew* their master *knew* he expected a return on his money and *knew* he expected them to *take some risk*. It seems these specific servants also sensed that the master *hoped* to see the servants take ownership and *was looking for ways* to trust them more. Those servants who perceived these items stepped embrace the challenge and met the master's expectations. These first two servants knew the master; they knew his expectations and they owned them. These two were rewarded for their efforts: the master doubled his trust in them.

However, the one who was judged had the following characteristics: he saw the master as hard and demanding (v. 24), the servant perceived the master to be unfair and unjust (v. 24), the servant was fearful of his master instead of trusting (v. 25), the servant avoided all risk because he didn't trust his master's heart if he failed (v. 25).

The master doesn't display the need to defend his self. It is here that I perceive the master to explain:

*If you really were afraid, then you should have done something, anything to be profitable that you believed had a risk that was acceptable to you and to me. You should have done something, anything with the investment I gave you. Doing nothing is infinitely worse than doing something with even the slightest risk. You should have found a way to represent me while I was gone. Burying what I gave you and giving it back was not an option, and if you really knew me, you'd have known that.*

Then in verses 28-30, we read:

*<sup>28</sup>Take therefore the talent from him, and give [it] unto him which hath ten talents. <sup>29</sup>For unto every one that hath shall be given, and he shall have abundance: but from him that hath not shall be taken away even that which he hath. <sup>30</sup>And cast ye the unprofitable servant into outer darkness: there shall be weeping and gnashing of teeth.*

Let's look specifically at verse 29. To everyone that "hath" shall be given and from him that "hath not" shall be taken. What could this mean? It cannot reference money or talents because they all had money and talents. It cannot represent opportunity because they all had opportunity. It cannot reference their favored position because all three were servants trusted by the master. It cannot represent the task at hand, because all three had the same task. The one thing that the two servants had that the one did not was an understanding of their master; a sense of his expectations; a trust in his empowerment; a fear of his judgment. In short, those who understood their master's heart are those that "hath" and those that "hath not" do not understand or know their master. It's notable that it was "their" master—all three of the servants had the same master; yet two knew their master and one did not, and the one that did not know his master and that did not *do what his master expected* was punished severely and called unprofitable:

*³⁰And cast ye the unprofitable servant into outer darkness: there shall be weeping and gnashing of teeth.*

Again, we see the severe punishment of not doing what is expected of the master: weeping and gnashing of teeth.

One last thought to share on this topic before moving forward. Do you find yourself looking at others and saying, "Man, they have so much. I wish I did. I don't feel like I have anything to offer God." If that is you, please consider my words. This parable shows that the master gave to each servant according to his trust and perception of them and their abilities. This is our call to look at what we have and to say: "I will be the most faithful servant Jesus has ever had with what I've got! I will not look at other servants and wish I had what they have: I will prove myself to Jesus with what I have, and I will make Him proud." That response works consistently irrespective of the level of trust you currently have with Jesus. That response honors His heart, His desire, His purpose for you and opens the door for Him to trust you even more. Do your best with what you have! Do something with what He's given you! Take some risk and trust the Master's heart toward you.

## How Did We Get Here?

Before we step into the final parable of Matthew 25, let's recall how we arrived here. The disciples started by asking Jesus, "When will these things happen? What is the sign of your coming? What is the sign of the end of the world?" For the last number of pages, we seem to have been focused on life skills! Did you get lost at any point and ask the question, "What does this have to do with the end times?" Likely, the disciples were thinking the same thing as they listened to

Jesus. The disciples asked Jesus: When will the temple be destroyed? What will be the sign of your coming? And what will be the sign of the end of the age? Then, Jesus begins to answer their question in a way they don't likely expect, starting with the words:

> *4...Take heed that no man deceive you.*

He then steps into the end-times sequence that begins with their current day and ends with the end of the world (Mt 24:14), only to circle back and start filling in details. The first and greatest detail appears to be the most pivotal event prior to Jesus appearing: the appearance of the abomination of desolation (Mt 24:15). From there, Jesus takes us again to the end of the age that culminates with the sun being darkened, the moon being darkened, the stars falling from heaven and the sign of the Son appearing in heaven (Mt 24:29) which will come as a surprise. After this, Jesus addresses how we must be ready for Him and how we should watch with vigilance and always be ready (Mt 24:36 forward), because at the sign of His appearing it will be too late to prepare.

How do we remain ready? We listen and prepare like Noah, we stay awake and guard our house like the goodman, we become the good servant who does his master's will while He's away, we come ready for however long it takes and we stay alert listening for the sound of his coming like the virgins, we take risk and invest whatever our master has given us while we wait because we know he expects a return on his investment and because He trusts us. Jesus spends more time explaining how to wait for Him than He does about how He will return, which tells me Jesus was not as concerned about the disciples knowing when He would return as He was with the importance of His disciples' focused preparation and readiness. Jesus gave the most important response to the disciples' questions, perhaps just not what they expected.

## Parable of the Sheep and Goats (Mt 25:31-46)

After all of this, Jesus punctuates His answer to the disciples with one final parable before ending His interaction on the topic of the end times: the parable of the sheep and the goats. Like before, let's read the entire parable and as we step into it, let's remember what Jesus has said so far, and that he's still answering the question "When shall these things be? What is the sign of your coming? What is the sign of the end of the age?" Matthew 25:31-46 records Jesus final words on the matter:

> [31]When the Son of man shall come in his glory, and all the holy angels with him, then shall he sit upon the throne of his glory: [32]And before him shall be gathered all nations: and he shall separate them one from another, as a shepherd divideth [his] sheep from the goats: [33]And he shall set the sheep on his right hand, but the goats on the left. [34]Then shall the King say unto them on his right hand, Come, ye blessed of my Father, inherit the kingdom prepared for you from the foundation of the world: [35]For I was an hungred, and ye gave me meat: I was thirsty, and ye gave me drink: I was a stranger, and ye took me in: [36]Naked, and ye clothed me: I was sick, and ye visited me: I was in prison, and ye came unto me.
>
> [37]Then shall the righteous answer him, saying, Lord, when saw we thee an hungred, and fed [thee]? or thirsty, and gave [thee] drink? [38]When saw we thee

*a stranger, and took [thee] in? or naked, and clothed [thee]? $^{39}$Or when saw we thee sick, or in prison, and came unto thee? $^{40}$And the King shall answer and say unto them, Verily I say unto you, Inasmuch as ye have done [it] unto one of the least of these my brethren, ye have done [it] unto me.*

$^{41}$*Then shall he say also unto them on the left hand, Depart from me, ye cursed, into everlasting fire, prepared for the devil and his angels: $^{42}$For I was an hungred, and ye gave me no meat: I was thirsty, and ye gave me no drink: $^{43}$I was a stranger, and ye took me not in: naked, and ye clothed me not: sick, and in prison, and ye visited me not.*

$^{44}$*Then shall they also answer him, saying, Lord, when saw we thee an hungred, or athirst, or a stranger, or naked, or sick, or in prison, and did not minister unto thee? $^{45}$Then shall he answer them, saying, Verily I say unto you, Inasmuch as ye did [it] not to one of the least of these, ye did [it] not to me. $^{46}$And these shall go away into everlasting punishment: but the righteous into life eternal.*

Jesus finally exclaims, after all that He's said so far, "When the Son of man shall come in his glory, and all the holy angels [envoys] with him, then shall he sit upon the throne of his glory..." (v. 31). This is different from the previous event of the sign of the Son of man in Mt 24:30. In Mt 24:30-31, there are not yet any people with Jesus, and it is at the sign of the Son that the elect are gathered by the angels. Here, the elect, human and angel, return with Jesus as He comes to take His kingdom and it is *now* that Jesus says He will sit on His throne. As we will see, this corresponds with Revelation 19, at the time Jesus returns to execute judgment on the earth.

Jesus answered the sign of His coming in Mt 24:29-31 and here Jesus is finally answering the disciples question: What will be the sign of the end of the age? Jesus tells us, yet once more, that His favor is dependent upon what we do and have done. All the nations of the earth are gathered before Him. He evaluates everyone, separating them into two groups: sheep and goats. Sheep are those who did the following: fed people, gave drink to people, invited in strangers, clothed naked, visited sick, and came to those in prison. Goats are those who did not do the following: they did not feed people, they did not give drink to people, they did not invite in strangers, they did not cloth the naked, they did not visit the sick, they did not come to those in prison.

Sheep on the right, goats on the left. Those who did on the right; those who did not on the left. The actions, in both cases, were done to people who were not Jesus Himself, but were other inhabitants of the earth. Jesus explains that doing any of these things to the least of the inhabitants of the earth is the same as doing it for Him. The person receiving the act does not need to be someone of importance, it can be anyone, beginning with the most unknown or undesirable person. The point Jesus is making here is the heart of the person doing the act. If we have a heart like His heart; if we love like He loves; if we intersect humanity the way He intersects humanity, then we are representing Him and representing His interests and we are adjudicated as "sheep." If we don't represent Him and His interests as if He were here Himself, if we don't express His actions and His heart, then we are adjudicated as "goats." The sheep are also known as the "righteous" (v. 37) and inherit the kingdom prepared for them by His father (v. 34). The goats are also known as "cursed" (v. 41) and inherit everlasting punishment and specifically "into everlasting fire, prepared for the devil and his angels" (v. 41).

We cannot dumb this down because we don't like what it says. If you are reading this and you are not doing what Jesus says, you fall into the "goat" category and judgment awaits. Our response to this should *not* be to say, "that doesn't apply to me because the blood of Jesus cleanses me of all sin." Jesus does not appear to talk about the power of His blood atonement, He is saying that the righteous will have these events in their life: these events will be valuable and important and existent in the life of a sheep. If these events are not in your life, you must question if you are a sheep.

There is time to change, and the decision must be yours. *You must choose.* The heart of the sheep and the heart of the goats is shown by their actions. Jesus has done everything he can already. Your salvation is not purchased by your works, but if you are not doing these things, Jesus challenges if you are a sheep. Those who are sheep will do these things, either naturally or by sheer decision out of love for the master; those who are goats will not.

From a practical sense, perhaps your asking, "How can I give a drink to someone? How can I visit someone in prison? I don't know any strangers and I sure wouldn't feel safe inviting one into my home. How am I supposed to do these things?" May I offer some thoughts? From the earlier parable of the talents, we saw that the master expected the servants to operate with some level of risk: we cannot play it safe and earn the Master's reward. Here are a few ways you might respond.

- Keep extra bottles of water within reach as you are in your car and when you see someone panhandling, give them some money and a bottle of water. I keep some spare bills in a container in my car console for this purpose. Will they abuse the money? Possibly, but that is between them and God.

- Ask your family and friends for someone who is in prison and start writing them if you cannot go physically. You can go to www.jailatm.com to try and find them.

- Would you like to see another prison? Go adopt people at a local nursing home. This is within your reach and welcomed by the nursing home staff.

- Go buy a bag of hamburgers or some hand warmers and hand them out to people in a lower income area if you live where people are on the streets.

- Drive around and look for strangers walking and ask if they need a ride somewhere.

- If you see someone asking for hand-outs, see if they need a tarp, a tent or something else. Most times, when I've asked, they only want money. If you don't want to give that, ask if they could use a gift card to a local fast-food restaurant and do that instead.

- When you see someone that needs a place to stay and you cannot invite them to stay in your home, consider purchasing them a hotel room for the night.

These are all things I've done personally to fulfill this Scripture in Matthew 25. Doing them means I give up personal time and money. For you, it may mean spending less or no money on boats and trucks; downsizing your home so you have money to invest in Jesus' kingdom; perhaps it means fewer vacations. If you're living on a low income already, perhaps it means you choose to fast a meal so you can give it away. Whatever it means to you, do it and if you don't want to do it, seriously ask God why and then change. I'd rather take the personal loss than to disobey or cheapen Jesus' trust in me. Again, remember, these are Jesus' words and our not liking them doesn't affect their truth. Finally, remember, **these are Jesus answers to the end-times questions; these are how Jesus tells us to be ready for His return and the end of the world.**

## Pulling It Together (Mt 25:1-46)

This is as uncomfortable to me as it is to you, believe me. We cannot explain away the truth of Scripture because we don't like what it says. We cannot say that the blood of Jesus is all we need to receive our eternal reward, when Jesus Himself is telling us in parable after parable that our actions matter, how we see Him matters, if we know His heart matters, if we are doing His heart matters, if we are making ourselves ready matters. Jesus blood atonement is the only way we will get into His kingdom, we can be made righteous no other way; but we cannot arrive into His kingdom with His blessing and favor without knowing and representing Him and His heart on earth; and our challenge to ourselves must be wrestling with the question: Am I really representing Jesus? Am I really bearing Him fruit? Am I really trying to produce for Him what he wants? How do I know? If I'm willing to look at Mt 24 and 25 and set it aside for my own convenience because it disagrees with what I've been taught, or because I don't think it applies to me. How do I know I'm right? Will I be a sheep? Will I be a goat?

Nothing in any of the parables of Mt 24 and Mt 25 gives the slightest inkling that a person is rewarded for their position as a favored servant. In *every case* the servants had to prove their selves. They had to prove they were what the master expected, that they represented Him well, that they respected and feared Him and that they knew His heart for them and for those of mankind. Nowhere in these teachings on the coming judgment and coming kingdom of Jesus do we see that merely being a goodman, a servant or a virgin attendant was enough to receive the blessing. Position had nothing to do with the reward except being a starting point for each person, giving them the chance to earn the right of blessing, and yes, I just said "earn"; and as we will soon see in the Revelation, we can surrender our Salvation by not living as Jesus expects, not meeting His requirements of servanthood and we can be cast into hell. Jesus just said that here in Matthew 25:41-45 and we see it again in the Revelation. Go read Revelation 3:5 as Jesus warns the churches if we do not overcome, He will blot out our name from the book of life, then go read Rev 20:15 that states,

*15And whosoever was not found written in the book of life was cast into the lake of fire.*

Jesus point is clear: we cannot say we are one thing and act as something else.

Can you see in Jesus' own words through Matthew 24 and 25 that our actions determine our outcomes? The grace of God is given to us through the blood of Jesus, and it covers a multitude of sins, but if we are not acting like Jesus on this earth and feeding His interests, we are in grave jeopardy of being judged with the hypocrites and being left outside of His presence. We may make it out of hell, but we will not make it out of judgment and out of sorrow for our abject failure to see what is important. Believe me when I say, our reward *is dependent* upon what we do and how we represent Him and His interests.

James, the ½ brother of Jesus, discusses this in the following section from James 2:18-26:

> *[18]Yea, a man may say, Thou hast faith, and I have works: shew me thy faith without thy works, and I will shew thee my faith by my works. [19]Thou believest that there is one God; thou doest well: the devils also believe, and tremble. [20]But wilt thou know, O vain man, that faith without works is dead? [21]Was not Abraham our father justified by works, when he had offered Isaac his son upon the altar? [22]Seest thou how faith wrought with his works, and by works was faith made perfect? [23]And the Scripture was fulfilled which saith, Abraham believed God, and it was imputed unto him for righteousness: and he was called the Friend of God. [24]Ye see then how that by works a man is justified, and not by faith only. [25]Likewise also was not Rahab the harlot justified by works, when she had received the messengers, and had sent [them] out another way? [26]For as the body without the spirit is dead, so faith without works is dead also.*

Pay special attention to verse 24, "Ye see then [James expects us to get this] how that by works a man is justified, and not by faith only." Friends, we *must* not just ascend to salvation because of grace. Grace is the opportunity to receive salvation, but without works to accompany the grace, our faith is useless and dead. Verse 26 says this specifically. Look at James 2:26:

> *26For as the body without the spirit is dead, so faith without works is dead also.*

We are saved by faith in Jesus. Without works to accompany the faith, we have *no faith!* It is dead. We can only have faith if it's accompanied by works. What has Jesus said over and over in Mt 24 and Mt 25? We are not rewarded or judged based on our position, on our calling or on who we are as servants or attendants: we are rewarded starting from that position only by *fulfilling a life of works.* Jesus said this. James is saying it here. We cannot have faith without works and have a living faith. Faith without accompanying works is dead.

Is your faith dead? How can you know? Allow the scriptures from Mt 24 and Mt 25 and James 2 to judge your heart. Are you convicted at heart that you're not doing what you should? Then do it. Are you convicted that you should do more? Then do it! Are you convicted that you're wasting your money on *stuff* when you should be giving more of it away to others? Then do it! Are you spending more money on vacations and object than you are Jesus' kingdom? If you are, just realize that you're receiving nothing outside of this life for those amounts. There is nothing wrong with enjoying the fruit of your labors, but if all you are doing is enjoying the fruit of your labors and you are not investing it into Jesus' kingdom, you are setting yourself up for an eternal failure.

If you are reading these words, there is still time for you to prove yourself to the Master before you see Him face to face: whether you go to Him, or He comes to you. Will you join me as we, together, ignite or rekindle our dedication to love Jesus, to love His heart, to love His desires, to serve His expectations, to fear Him and to strive to prove ourselves to Him? Will you join me in dedicating yourself to these outcomes so that we have living faith? So that we have faith that is proven and that ushers us into the category of sheep and not goats; so that as we enter His kingdom, we are treated with honor and not judged as hypocrites? This, Jesus says, is the most important part of His coming.

# Matthew 24 and 25: the Backdrop

The reason I started with Matthew 24 and Matthew 25 as the backdrop for the Revelation and Daniel are because Jesus is the Word of God, and His perspective of the end times is what matters. We have learned from Jesus that for us to be ready for the sign of His coming and His final return, we have work to do. We must be prepared, we must expect Him, we must invest our lives in His expected outcomes, we must know Him and His heart, we must fear Him and we must realize that He will reward us and punish us based on how we live for His expected outcomes. These are the take-away points Jesus says are the most important answers to the questions of His return and the end of the age. It's not that His appearing and return are unimportant or less important; however, Jesus knows how we are living before His return will affect us most at His return; and His heart is to honor and reward us as we enter the kingdom of His Father. Jesus seems to be saying:

*My return is coming, and it will be the greatest event in the history of humankind since My resurrection, but what makes it so defining is how you will be found when it happens. When I come, it will be too late to change. When I come, it will be too late to begin caring. When I come it will be too late to prove yourself. You must do all those things now, before I come, so that at my coming I can reward you for your faithfulness. Will you live for me so I can reward you? My return will be a one moment event, but your preparation is a lifetime. Will you take this seriously, please? Because I want you to have faith that is living, I want you to have blessing that is eternal, I want you in my Father's kingdom as close to me as you can come, but only you can prove yourself worthy of all these. My death and resurrection opened the door, now you must forge the journey to receive the depth and breadth of the blessings of My kingdom. Will you dedicate yourself to my heart and purpose in your life and prove your faith with works worthy of reward?*

For the record, the last paragraph was fully my own writing, but as I walk away from Mt 24 and 25, and as I apply all that we will soon see in the Revelation, this is how I summarize it; and as we walk next into the Revelation of Jesus, will you join me in this prayer?

*God, please help us to find what is honest and true in your eyes. Help us see that this world is not what we think and that we must be about your business. Help us see and find the opportunities around us that need filled. Help us see people and needs and give us eyes to step into the works you would do if you were here. Help us not be complacent or distracted or faithless, but help us do what you would do, when you would do it, with and to those you see with your heart and mind and in an honest and trusting fear of your judgment and final decision. Help us prove ourselves worthy of the grace you've given us and to prove to you that the faith you have placed in us, and into which you have allowed us to walk, is alive and active. God place us in Jesus and Jesus in us and let us walk in Him as His body while He is away. Amen.*

Are you ready for what is next?  The coming pages are filled with the amazing and we get to encounter them together.  Revelation and Daniel, here we come!

# Notes

# Index

## N

Nah 3:3, 88
nah-os', 72
nation
    against nation, 20, 26, 27
nations of earth, 158
Nero Caesar, 117, See also:
    Caesar:Nero
Noah, 123, 124, 138, 139, 141,
    155
Noah daughters, 125
Noah sons, 125
normal vs truth, 17
Num 14:29-33, 88
nursing baby, 61
nursing mothers, 58

## O

o-deen', 22, 23
ōdin, 23
offended, 31, See skandalizō
on'-om-ah, 21
oo-ran-os', 101
or-gay, 53
our actions, 162
our outcomes, 162

## P

pangs, birth, 23
parable
    fig tree, 104, 107, 141
    good man, 141
    Noah, 141
    servant, 141
    sheep and goats, 156
    sheep and the goats, 156
    talents, of the, 148
    tares, 130

Ten Virgins, 142
    virgins, ten, 140
pas, 31
Paul, 10, 11, 12, 23, 116, 120
peace and safety, 23
peh'gher, 88
perceptions, 18, 68
perdition
    son of, 11
persecution, 27, 81, 82
persevere, 40
pestilence, 20, 23, 27
Pikuach nefesh, 63
plagues, 23
poor, the, 19
Porcius Festus, 116
position of trust, 144
poverty, 16
powers of heaven
    shaken, 92
pregnant, 80
prepare
    failure to, 75
prepared, 146, 166
pretender, 137
pro, 27
prophets
    false, 32
Ps 110:6, 88
psoo'-kho, 33
pto'-mah, 90

## R

rapture. See elect:gathering, See:
    catching away
reality
    perception, 16
redemption, 39
remain, 113
reproof, 89

Made in the USA
Coppell, TX
13 December 2022

89124750R00105